12 ANGRY MEN

12
ANGRY MEN

TRUE STORIES OF BEING
A BLACK MAN IN AMERICA TODAY

EDITED BY

GREGORY S. PARKS

AND

MATTHEW W. HUGHEY

WITH AN INTRODUCTION BY
LANI GUINIER

THE NEW PRESS
NEW YORK
LONDON

Requests for permission to reproduce selections from this book should be mailed to: Permissions Department, The New Press, 38 Greene Street, New York, NY, 10013.

Part of chapter 3 is excerpted from *Joe Morgan: A Life in Baseball* by Joe Morgan and David Falkner (1993) and is reprinted with the permission of W.W. Norton & Company, Inc.

Chapter 11 is excerpted from *It's Bigger Than Hip-Hop* by M.K. Asante Jr. (2008) and is reprinted with the permission of St. Martin's Press.

Published in the United States by The New Press, New York, 2010
Distributed by Perseus Distribution

LIBRARY OF CONGRESS CATALOGING-IN-PUBLICATION DATA

12 angry men : true stories of being a black man in America today / edited by Gregory S. Parks and Matthew W. Hughey.
    p. cm.
  Includes bibliographical references.
  ISBN 978-1-59558-538-7 (hc. : alk. paper) 1. African American men--Attitudes--History--21st century. 2. Racial profiling in law enforcement--United States. 3. United States--Race relations. 4. African Americans--Social conditions--21st century. 5. Racism--United States. I. Parks, Gregory, 1974- II. Hughey, Matthew W. (Matthew Windust) III. Title: Twelve angry men.
  E185.615.A12 2010
  305.896'07300922--dc22

2010032244

The New Press was established in 1990 as a not-for-profit alternative to the large, commercial publishing houses currently dominating the book publishing industry. The New Press operates in the public interest rather than for private gain, and is committed to publishing, in innovative ways, works of educational, cultural, and community value that are often deemed insufficiently profitable.

www.thenewpress.com

Composition by The Influx House
This book was set in Galliard

Printed in the United States of America

10 9 8 7 6 5 4 3 2 1

To the memory of Oscar Grant, Sean Bell,
Amadou Diallo, and the countless brothers who have
lost their lives, and dignity, to racial profiling

CONTENTS

12 ANGRY MEN

INTRODUCTION

FROM RACIAL PROFILING TO RACIAL LITERACY: LESSONS OF 12 ANGRY MEN

LANI GUINIER

The phrase "Twelve Angry Men" is rife with current meaning. Film buffs will remember that, in the Sidney Lumet classic, ethnic bias figured starkly in the all-white jury's initial, knee-jerk conclusion of guilt. Anger animated the other jurors' reaction when Henry Fonda's character used doubt and reason to resist their prejudice. This black-and-white depiction of America certainly still resonates.

Now, nearly six decades later, the tables have been turned: the men who are angry in this *12 Angry Men* are the accused themselves—the stopped-and-frisked, the unlawfully detained, the racially profiled. These men's accounts of their interactions with the police are cinematic in their clarity and pathos. Their anger is understandable, justifiable. It stems from an often arbitrary, sometimes violent moment of encounter with personified state power, with its attendant embarrassment, helplessness, and fear. That anger also reflects the long chain of confrontation in this country between institutionalized state power and the individual, particularly the individual of color.

In this book are the actual voices of African American men across a spectrum of society, decrying the ugly, thoughtless, terrifying rejection of their individuality, the spasmodic yet ancient focus of authority on one all-too-frequently-invoked presumption: you are black, so the burden is on you to prove that you are not dangerous. As baseball great Joe Morgan relates in his account of being racially profiled by a member of the LAPD at the Los Angeles airport, even celebrity is no exception to what we can consider the inverse of color blindness.

Racial profiling is a reality that we often don't hear mentioned in the Obama era, because liberal and conservative pundits alike tell us that we now live in a post-racial America. Or we are cautioned that to speak up about race is itself an act of racism. Thus, the gripping racial profiling stories of twelve black men represent an important rejoinder to contemporary post-racial admonitions. Their stories are eloquent reminders that race, as in racial profiling, still matters.

According to the ACLU, racial profiling is "the use of race by law enforcement in any fashion and to any degree when making decisions about whom to stop, interrogate, search, or arrest—except where there is a specific suspect description" that includes the suspect's race. This is the "technical" definition, focused on law enforcement excesses. In its daily manifestations, racial profiling by law enforcement provides a pattern of situations and locations and a standard cast of characters that are as predictable as a Christmas pageant: police officers stop young men of color for walking-while-black, driving-while-black, flying-while-black, and, in the case of *New York Times* reporter Solomon Moore, even reporting-while-black. Black men are not the only objects of racial profiling, but they are the most profiled group in the country.

The contributors to *12 Angry Men* tell firsthand stories representative of each of these forms of profiling. Congressman Daniel K. Davis and the young artist and professor M.K. Asante tell of being behind the wheel of a car pulled over by the police and subjected to a degrading kind of treatment, based on a presumption of guilt that few white Americans ever experience. The former head of the ACLU's racial profiling division, who was himself profiled at Boston's Logan Airport coming home from a racial profiling conference, describes how airports are also fertile ground for this pernicious practice (and increasingly for the profiling of black women suspected of drug couriering). Leaving a bar or a club is also a defining moment for police encounters, according to Bryonn Bain, my former student at Harvard Law School, and aspiring hip-hop artist Joshua T. Wiley, a native of Asheville, North Carolina, both of whom recount their experiences here.

Evidently, for many young black men all that matters is the color of their skin, regardless of the place or time, as Nii-Odoi Glover, an event marketer in Los Angeles, makes painfully clear. When he was a teenager in Washington, D.C., Glover recounts:

> the cops would stop me and my friends and verbally harass us about where we were going and what we were doing—all under the pretense that they were "looking for someone that fits your

description." This was the socialization that we went through. Even though we came from diverse backgrounds, were of various ages, and had various levels of education, we were all stopped and harassed regularly by the cops.

Then, in his twenties, driving to and from work, Glover was pulled over repeatedly:

> I got stopped at least once a month, sometimes three times a month. My roommate at the time was aware of the situation and understood that if he was to ride anywhere with me, then we had to plan to leave early enough to account for the time spent if we were to be stopped. We would try to make a joke out of it: "Here come your boys!" he would say when cops behind us would turn on their sirens.

And now, as a grown man and a father, Glover draws police attention for reading a book in the playground while supervising his daughter at play: "[The police] told me that someone called them and told them that 'a black man was in the park watching kids.'"

Racial profiling has been such a dominant phenomenon coursing through our history that it does not take long for those coming to the United States from other countries to learn the rules. Devon W. Carbado, now a law professor and one of the contributors to this book, emigrated to the United States from England as a young man. About a year after he arrived he purchased his first car, a used yellow convertible. Within two weeks of this purchase, while driving in Inglewood, a predominantly black neighborhood south of Los Angeles, Carbado and his brother were stopped and searched, spread-eagled on the side of a police cruiser. At first the cops were confused by the brothers' British accents, but soon regained their composure. As Carbado explains in his essay, "Notes of a Naturalized Son," the officers quickly convicted the young men using the body of "uncontestable" evidence—their race. Just as quickly, the brothers realized that they "were one step closer to becoming black Americans."

We might well expect in our era of presumed color-blind enlightenment that police and their law enforcement bosses would deny that race is a likely marker of guilt. But we would be wrong. The NYPD's highly touted Commissioner Raymond W. Kelly, among other officials, has shamelessly justified the enormous racial disproportionality of profiling practices (of the 575,000 New Yorkers stopped in 2009 in accordance with the NYPD's stop-and-frisk policy, 89 percent were black or Latino) based on the assertion that empirically blacks commit more crimes. Scholars directly dispute this assertion. More important, they point out that in most instances police don't know the race of the person they are chasing and thus cannot legitimately use that as a basis for suspicion.[1] Indeed, young men such as nineteen-year-old Richard F. of East Harlem, who is routinely stopped and searched by the police, understand intuitively the meaningless nature of the phrase "reasonable suspicion":

> If I ask [the police] why they are searching me, they just make up a reason. They lie. Let's say I have on a red sweater. They might say someone with a red sweater was reported for doing something—a lie so that they can search me or my friends. I know that it isn't legal for them to search me for no reason, but they can just say I look suspicious. I've tried to speak up and

tell them they can't search me, but they say they
don't care. So I just let them. What's the point?
If I try to argue with them, there are going to
be more cops coming. For questioning what
they say, there will be a whole pile of cops in my
building, just for me.

Within the twelve stories in this book lie surprising yet common seams of truth. First, racial profiling
as a law enforcement practice is ubiquitous. Second, it
is a bad law enforcement practice. It is also bad public
policy. Racial profiling is the thin end of the wedge of
our misuse of the criminal justice system as a major
instrument of urban social policy. Third, racial profiling is a widespread practice that is not limited to law
enforcement. Instead, racial profiling is like secondhand smoke that circulates invisibly in dark, closed
spaces. Racial profiling is pervasive (at least in part)
because the commonplace association of black people
with danger exerts a powerful yet often imperceptible
influence on the operation of the unconscious minds
of many Americans, not just those who work in law
enforcement. Finally, a political culture that discour-
ages us from learning how to "read" race in its con-

temporary context disables us from understanding how racial profiling, like secondhand smoke, currently pollutes our collective consciousness. In sum, we need less racial profiling and more racial literacy.

RACIAL PROFILING IS UBIQUITOUS

Racial or ethnic profiling—the practice of using group characteristics as a proxy for suspicion—is widespread. As the stories in this book reveal, racial profiling promiscuously afflicts black men. But its targets are not only black men. The long chain of confrontation between institutionalized state power and individuals of color not only dehumanized Africans imported in shackles and sold at auctions, but it also displaced and uprooted Native Americans. It continued with laws passed in the nineteenth century refusing laundry permits to the same Chinese immigrants who helped build the transcontinental railroad and in the twentieth century with the internment of 120,000 law-abiding Japanese Americans during World War II. The ugliness of this massive detention of Japanese American families was officially recognized as racial profiling in the Civil Liberties Act of 1988 and subsequently in

President Bill Clinton's letter to the victims, formally apologizing for actions that "were rooted deeply in racial prejudice, war time hysteria and the lack of political leadership."

Racial profiling continues to affect those whom hyphens or status categorizes: "illegals," "terrorist-sympathizers," "gang-bangers." Arizona has provided us with a new category that we can call "looking Mexican." The governor signed a law in April 2010 that, if enforced, would require police to stop and question anyone arousing a "reasonable suspicion" of not having proper immigration papers. The current frenzy to pass similar anti-immigrant laws, if successful, has the potential both to create a tangled web of local rules and to legitimate the widespread profiling of American citizens of Hispanic descent.

Arab Americans have already been detained in indiscriminate and haphazard post-9/11 dragnets. The events of September 11 and its aftermath have led to "flying while Muslim," which in one notorious instance focused law enforcement on an Orthodox Jewish youth who was praying on an airplane. These officially sanctioned moments of encounter span landscapes of vast geographical, racial, and ethnic dimensions. Amnesty International estimates that 32 million Americans have reported being victims of these practices and 87 million Americans are at high risk of being profiled in the future.[2]

RACIAL PROFILING IS BAD LAW ENFORCEMENT AS WELL AS BAD PUBLIC POLICY

In Brownsville, Brooklyn, from 2006 to 2010, a small army of New York City rookie cops, just out of police school, blanketed a roughly eight-block rectangle of apartment buildings and public housing projects every night. During a four-year period, the police stopped 52,000 people in this tough, majority-black Brooklyn neighborhood, logging names of those stopped into a police database, although most were not arrested (the arrest rate was less than 1 percent of those stopped). According to the *New York Times*, "The officers stop people they think might be carrying guns; they stop and question people who merely enter the public housing project buildings without a key; they ask for identification from, and run warrant checks on, young people halted for riding bicycles on the sidewalk."[3] The frequency of the stops hits young men aged fifteen to thirty-four especially hard. They represent 11 percent of the area's population and 68 percent of those who are stopped. Jonathan Guity, a twenty-six-year-old legal assistant with no criminal record, grew up in this community and still lives there. Guity was asked by a *New York Times* reporter how often he has been stopped in the last four years. Without skipping a beat, Guity responded. "Honestly, I'd say thirty to forty times. I'm serious."

Those who live in this gritty urban neighborhood welcome the police, but they are increasingly ambivalent about the stop-and-frisk policy's effects. Even senior citizens express growing uneasiness at the high chance of getting stopped at any time. Longtime residents watch with dismay as the rookie cops have trouble distinguishing the black kid wearing baggy pants on his way home from school from another young man in low-hanging jeans carrying a concealed weapon. "Young black men get stopped so often that a few years ago, Gus Cyrus, coach of the football team at nearby Thomas Jefferson High School, started letting his players leave practice with their bright orange helmets so the police would not confuse them with gang members," reported the *Times*.[4]

Brownsville old-timers grumble that the young officers don't try to build relationships or take advantage of local expertise. The rookie cops "seem to be more interested in small offenses than engaging with residents." According to Richard Rosenfeld, a professor of criminology and criminal justice, stop-and-frisks that do not result in arrests can also warp the community's confidence in the police and can undermine the ability of the police to do their jobs well.[5]

Relationships are important; so is trust. Cooperation with law enforcement plummets—in Brownsville and beyond—when residents feel degraded by arbitrary and humiliating interactions with cops. Kent H., a thirty-five-year-old father and former job counselor, was born and raised in the Bronx. In "Severed Ties," he graphically describes his multiple racial profiling experiences—from sitting in a park in the projects where he lived minding his own business and talking on his cell phone to charges of "trespassing" because he dared to visit a friend in his friend's building. His rage is especially visceral and percussive as he recalls a nightmarish strip search by four D.T.'s (New York City detectives). He was inside the lobby of his own building in the Bronx talking with a friend when the D.T.'s ran in screaming

"Get your hands on the fucking wall! Get your hands up; hands on the wall!" . . . Four big white guys pulled down our pants—the whole nine yards. Supposedly because they felt we had drugs on us. They were saying, "We know you got drugs on you. We're going to find 'em."

It was the most embarrassing experience. People were coming in the lobby and they saw this happen. It was crazy, really crazy. When they realized that we didn't have anything, they just left. No apologies, no "I'm sorry"—nothing, nothing, nothing! They just left us standing there. They walked away and we put our clothes back on.

Kent H. doesn't think all cops are bad. "But the majority are. . . . They abuse their power to the fullest extent."

Ultimately, cops risk missing the bad guy when they profile the black guy—and definitely give the black guy good cause not to help catch that same bad guy. It's lose-lose law enforcement, as the following statistics make clear:

- A 1999 Justice Department study found that, while police officers disproportionately stopped and searched African American and Latino automobile drivers, whites possessed illegal drugs more often (17 percent of the time) than blacks (8 percent) when they were searched.

- 2009 data provided by the NYPD under a court order and analyzed by the Center for Constitutional Rights shows that, according to the *New York Times*, "Blacks and Latinos were nine times as likely as Whites to be stopped by the police in New York City in 2009 but, once stopped, were no more likely to be arrested."

- Another study in New Jersey determined that state troopers found drugs in automobiles driven by whites 25 percent of the time, by blacks 13 percent, and by Latinos 5 percent.[6]

- When the U.S. Customs Service eliminated racial profiling as a method for detecting smuggling, the productivity of searches increased by 300 percent.[7]

Racial profiling also flies in the face of basic constitutional values, international law protocols, and the fundamental commitment of our democracy to equality and fairness.[8] In 1968 the U.S. Supreme Court ruled that police may stop and frisk people based on a "reasonable suspicion" of danger, short of the probable cause that warrants arrest. However, the Court subsequently specified that race or ethnicity could not itself be the basis of such reasonable suspicion. What the Court in later years has made it quite difficult to do is *prove* that a police officer stopped or searched someone based on race. Short of the officer's admission of such a racist rationale, there is little way to challenge police conduct as discriminatory. However, this convenient procedural constraint on asserting civil rights does not justify the underlying conduct. Racial profiling violates our basic constitutional norms even if jurisprudentially it is nearly impossible to prove.

In poor urban communities all over the United States, racial profiling continues mostly unabated. Yet racial profiling is not just about race. It is also about power and socioeconomic class. The correlation between race, poverty, and profiling is overwhelming. As William A. "Sandy" Darity Jr., a professor of public policy, African and African-American studies, and economics at Duke University, has reminded us, black people and Latinos still suffer from crushing gaps in wealth that are intergenerational, not personal, and are, in comparison to the white population, truly mind-boggling.[9] For example, Darity has pointed out that, according to 2002 data, the median white household has a net worth of $90,000, a Latino household has a net worth of only $8,000, and a black household has a net worth of just $6,000. Black people with a net worth of $6,000 "would have to save 100 percent of their income for three consecutive years," Darity says, to close the racial wealth gap, a gap that is the direct result of hundreds of years of slavery and Jim Crow.

Neighborhood poverty then cements the historic wealth gap. Continuing racial segregation—which isolates both middle-class and poor black people in high-poverty, high-crime neighborhoods—reinforces the gap. Even now, the children of middle-class black parents who have good jobs but live in poor neighborhoods experience downward economic mobility through no fault of their own. According to a 2009 study by the Pew Charitable Trusts, neighborhood poverty outweighed parents' education, employment, or marital status in explaining increases in black poverty. The study found that black children born between 1985 and 2000 are ten times more likely than white children to grow up in neighborhoods with a poverty rate of at least 20 percent. The same study found that half of black children born between 1955 and 1970 in middle-class families (those with incomes of $62,000 or higher in today's dollars) grew up in high-poverty neighborhoods, while almost no white middle-income children grew up in poor areas.

That finding is important, because it is the physical association between black people and poverty that contributes to cognitive assumptions about black criminality and results in the disproportionate attention that black males of all income levels receive from the police. Witness "Do You Live in this Neighborhood?," this book's story by Professor Paul Butler, a former prosecutor, who describes being followed home by the police in his upscale, mixed-race neighborhood of Washington, D.C. The police simply could not believe that he lived there. Bear in mind, then, Harvard Law student Bryonn Bain's "lesson in law," included in this book as "The Bill of Rights for Black Men." At the end of a weekend visiting family in New York City,

Bain had gone to the Latin Quarter and then stopped at a bodega in Manhattan to get some food. As Bain, his brother, and his cousin exited the store, armed only with sandwiches and Snapple, all three were accosted by the police and brusquely pushed up against a wall, "the legs of [their] dignity spread apart." The pat-down, arrest, and subsequent overnight detention uncovered nothing other than Bain's laptop, his Harvard ID, and a couple of law books he had intended to read on the bus ride back to Cambridge. Upon the discovery of these items, the arresting officer snickered that Bain must be at Harvard Law School on a "ball scholarship."

We don't have to imagine what would happen to well-to-do whites in similar circumstances. Consider, for example, the extraordinary cordiality of federal and state law enforcement authorities as they ramp up their investigation of illegal drugs on an elite college campus in Portland, Oregon, in the early spring of 2010. First, the local U.S. attorney pays a courtesy call on the president of Reed College to urge him to take steps to reduce the distribution and consumption of illegal drugs on the campus. Second, the law enforcement authorities focus on the "big-businessification of the illegal drug trade"—the dealers, not the upper-middle-class drug users.[10] The police explain in an e-mail message to students that the new market that drug dealers are targeting "is you." Unlike the black men of similar age who have been the primary objects of demeaning stop-and-frisks in Brownsville, Brooklyn, for the last four years, middle- and upper-class college students in Portland are politely informed via e-mail that they are not law enforcement's intended quarry. Third, the police forewarn the Reed College student body about possible undercover activity at an upcoming campus festival.

Middle-class college students who use drugs are seen as *victims*, not criminals, even though studies show that almost half of all college students (47.5 percent as of 2007, according to a study by the Office of National Drug Control Policy) have used illegal drugs. Indeed, the War on Drugs is generally not fought on bucolic college campuses or even in those middle-class predominantly white suburbs where drug use is widespread.[11] We might even say that this War on Drugs, which since the 1980s has been sustained through Republican and Democratic administrations and has contributed mightily to this nation's shocking explosion of incarceration, is arguably a case study of racial profiling and power run amok. Blacks do not use drugs more than whites but are arrested, prosecuted, convicted, and imprisoned on drug charges with ever greater concentration throughout the criminal justice process.[12]

In Obama's America, many of us assert with pride that a black man lives in the White House. At the same time, over two million Americans spend their days and nights in prisons or jails, a half million on drug charges. Nearly one million of those incarcerated are black. As Doug Massey and LiErin Probasco write in the *Du Bois Review*, black men, especially those with college degrees, are becoming so scarce that "one third of all black female college graduates will not be able to find a male partner unless they look outside the group or down the educational distribution, and among those graduating from selective colleges and universities, the majority of women cannot realistically hope to find a Black male partner of comparable education."[13]

Where, you might ask, are all the black men? Too many of them are in prison or jail. The United States has 5 percent of the world's population and 25 percent of the world's prisoners. Professor Butler states the dynamic succinctly: if the only tool you have is prison, every problem looks like a crime. The results are manifest in a system of racialized mass incarceration, one of our nation's greatest shames and contemporary burdens.

Yet racial profiling and racialized mass incarceration impact all Americans, not just people of color. If we begin to read race more carefully, we might learn that the conditions of profiling in the criminal justice system often affect blacks and Latinos first and most acutely, but that the same overreliance on the criminal justice system to police the black poor can disempower poor and working-class white people as well. Here I am referring to the fact that the white poor are overrepresented in prisons and jails because the school-to-prison pipeline also affects poor rural white men. The lack of a robust economic stimulus program to combat Depression-level unemployment within the black community also affects rising unemployment within many predominantly white counties in the Midwest. Or consider the higher rates of life-threatening conditions like diabetes, high blood pressure, and heart attacks among black and Latino men—which are actually a signal that we need to pay more attention to the health care crisis that is exacerbated by the anger, hopelessness, and diet in poor urban and rural communities around the country. And while close to one-third of black households have no or a negative net worth, Professor Darity points out that the same is true for 13 percent of white households.

RACIAL PROFILING IS *NOT* LIMITED
TO LAW ENFORCEMENT

Just as racial profiling is about the profiling of black men based, in part, on assumptions linking race and class, it is a practice that is not narrowly confined to law enforcement. The term racial profiling may have been coined to describe the behavior of cops on the beat and troopers on the state highways, yet Americans of all colors, including blacks, Latinos, Asians, and whites, still too readily associate random images of black people with images of bad people and pictures of unfamiliar white faces with pictures of friendly faces and pleasant words. Remember, even President Obama's white grandmother was a secret "racial profiler" in the colloquial—not law enforcement—sense of the term. She was the "woman who helped raise" him, "a woman who sacrificed again and again" for him, a woman who loved him "as much as she love[d] anything in this world, but a woman who once confessed her fear of black men who passed by her on the street, and who on more than one occasion has uttered racial or ethnic stereotypes that made [the young Obama] cringe."

Many of us continue to associate blacks with dangerousness, as reflected in the choices we make regarding where to live, where to send our children to school, where to shop, and when it is safe to venture out alone at night. Those choices are familiar, yet their unspoken relationship to racial hierarchies is rarely acknowledged. This negative association of blacks and danger is especially salient when we make snap judgments. And yet our minds—and our shared cultural narratives—help us hide these biases even from ourselves.

A recently developed test, the Implicit Association Test (IAT), offers one attempt to measure the extent of hidden bias. The IAT compares the speed by which the test takers pair certain words and images with each other. Millions of Americans have now taken the IAT; a majority show "implicit bias."[14] Implicit bias means that the test takers demonstrate much greater ease in associating good or friendly words like "pleasant" or "joy" with anonymous white faces and bad words like "dangerous" or "fear" with random black faces. One of the psychologists involved in developing the test, Tony Greenwald, says that when he took an early iteration of the IAT, he had as much difficulty pairing African American names "with pleasant words" as he did pairing "insect names with pleasant words." Similarly, Dr. Mahzarin Banaji, another one of the test's developers, was surprised by her own results. A self-described "progressive" and a person of color who holds no conscious bias, she found the test "difficult" and was "deeply embarrassed" with her own test results.[15]

The IAT outcomes remind us that our imperfect and race-conscious history continues to impose its collective weight on the way many of us think, despite our good intentions. The undisputed historical backdrop for racial profiling is two hundred and forty years of chattel slavery, a hundred years of Jim Crow, and four-hundred-plus years of intergenerational wealth transfer during which most of the time black people not only owned little property but *were* property. In roughly fifty of the first seventy-two years of our country's first century, the presidents of the United States themselves owned slaves. In the infamous Dred Scott case, in which the U.S. Supreme Court declared that a black man had no rights that a white man need respect, five of the justices were from slaveholding families.

This history may seem long ago, but it has left its thumbprint on our unconscious mental processes. Teachers, journalists, politicians, and ordinary citizens of all races find themselves unwittingly participating in a kabuki dance of racial profiling.[16] Whether we are white or black, Latino or Asian, we internalize that history's indelible impression, quickly though subconsciously pairing black faces with words like danger or with pictures of a weapon.[17] According to Dr. Banaji, we make these snap judgments in response to the "mindbugs" implanted by our history and our culture.

These mindbugs help explain the gaps between our words and our deeds. For example, on February 27, 2001, President George W. Bush opined that "racial profiling is wrong" and vowed to "end it in America." A little more than two years later, his Justice Department banned federal law enforcement agencies from practicing racial profiling, but with a standard exception for "national security" investigations and a just-as-typical lack of either enforcement mechanisms or data collection requirements. In August 2005, the Bush Justice Department tacked in the opposite direction, demoting the head of the Bureau of Justice Statistics for refusing to comply with a more senior official's order that he downplay in a press release the findings of a department study on racial profiling by police officers.

The Obama administration began with its own high hopes and big promises. Attorney General Eric Holder told Congress on May 7, 2009, that ending racial profiling was a "priority" and later added in a television interview that he himself had been a victim of this practice. Then, of course, came the infamous front-porch confrontation of Harvard professor Henry Louis Gates Jr., who is black, and Cambridge police sergeant James Crowley, who is white. The professor was a friend of Barack Obama, and the sergeant, a mentor of younger cops, had conducted diversity training. Both men were soon to become the president's beer buddies.

When a neighbor on Gates's tree-lined street reported what might be a prowler, the police handcuffed the fifty-eight-year-old, who walks with a cane, and arrested him for disorderly conduct on his own front porch. A June 2010 report commissioned by the city of Cambridge did not try to assess blame, but it pointed out the ways in which both Professor Gates, a prominent African American studies scholar, and Sergeant Crowley, an experienced officer, were reading and experiencing race differently. Crowley failed to "change his attitude toward Professor Gates" even after he realized that Gates posed no physical threat. In Gates's case, the commission concluded that he made the mistake of daring to talk back to the police, after taking offense that he was being mistaken for a burglary suspect in his own home. Just before he was led away in handcuffs by the police, and after he had shown his Harvard identification to the officer, Professor Gates reportedly said, "This is what happens to black men in America." Hollywood could not have asked for a more cinematic display of the many ways we each "read" race against the backdrop of history, culture, and our individual capacity to exercise power or wield authority.

FROM RACIAL PROFILING TO RACIAL LITERACY

Perhaps, the most important lesson of *12 Angry Men* is that Americans of all races and ethnicities need to become racially literate, not post-racially blind. Racial literacy is the capacity to "read" race, conjugate its grammar and interpret its meaning in different contexts and circumstances. All Americans, not just people of color, need to be better schooled in the subtle yet complex ways that racial profiling actually works in the twenty-first century.

For example, race is both a noun and a verb. In this sense it is like the words "profile" and "text." We read a text, but we also can text someone. Our faces may be observed from one side in "profile" but we also can profile or categorize other people. Similarly, we can read race as merely a superficial or fixed thing, such as skin color. We can also "race" someone as dangerous or as competent in a particular context, using race to code what we subconsciously believe are their intentions or their capacities. We "race" other people by our actions; we can also claim a race for ourselves. Or not. Like the verb "to be," race also takes a different form when we speak about "I am" versus "you are," compared with "he is."

As with any language, the language and grammar of race influence how we see and understand the world. As a result, the multiple meanings and uses of race need to be interrogated and conjugated carefully in light of relevant local circumstances and their historic underpinnings. For example, racial literacy demands a far more nuanced approach than typical charges of individual bigotry or intentional group prejudice.[18] Racial literacy, in other words, reads the grammar of racial profiling as a form of passive smoke. It reminds us that race is literally in the air we breathe and in the history that lives in our heads.

The secondhand smoke of racial profiling directly affects those in packed, close quarters defined by poverty and joblessness. It affects the young cops sent into unfamiliar neighborhoods by majors and chiefs of police focusing on statistics and quick fixes. It also insinuates its effects on those who observe the encounter replayed from a physical, though not necessarily psychic, distance on a TV watched in the privacy of a den or on a closed-circuit video from the jury box in a courtroom.

Racial literacy would help all of us understand that behind the two force fields competing for respect in the profiling moment—civil order and individual liberty—is a criminal justice system that exercises outsized power and responsibility as the major urban policy instrument for controlling the poor. At the same time, we have too often put our police officers into the positions of legislators, prosecutors, judges, and juries—positions for which they are not qualified and that they should not be expected to fulfill—even in well-to-do neighborhoods.

This book of stories by black men living in America can serve as a primer to help all Americans understand the dominant roles that history and culture, race, and intergenerational poverty all play in defining how we enforce our laws. Most of all, the twelve angry men remind us of the outsized role that we give to law enforcement in running our lives. Race, in the profiling context, is a convenient, powerful, and dangerous category; it easily morphs into other categories of class and criminality. These perceptual and social constructions of ours become political and legal. Yet they are also ignored because we lack a grammar or vocabulary for talking about them. Not surprisingly then, we find ourselves trapped, looking at each other through bars fixed by our unconscious acceptance of these constructions.

If we "read race" through the eyes and the pain of these twelve angry men, we can begin to see through the bars. We become familiar with the grammar of racial literacy and the text and the subtext of racial profiling. We learn that the conversation on race continues in a new space. It has moved from the "colored" water fountain and the back of the bus to the profiling moment and the prison cell.

NOTES

1. See Al Baker, "Lawsuit Challenges Stop-and-Frisk Database," *New York Times* City Room Blog, May 19, 2010, http://cityroom .blogs.nytimes.com/2010/05/19/lawsuit-challenges-stop-and -frisk-database/.
2. "Threat and Humiliation: Racial Profiling, National Security, and Human Rights in the United States," Amnesty International USA report, 2004, http://www.amnestyusa.org/us-human-rights/ other/rp-report----threat-and-humiliation/page.do?id=1106664.
3. Ray Rivera, Al Baker, and Janet Roberts, "A Few Blocks, 4 Years, 52,000 Police Stops," *New York Times*, July 11, 2010, http://www .nytimes.com/2010/07/12/nyregion/12frisk.html.
4. Ibid.
5. Ibid.

6. "Racial Profiling: The Truth About Racial Profiling: Seven Facts," Amnesty International USA, http://www.amnestyusa.org/racial_profiling/sevenfacts.html.

7. "Racial Profiling Doesn't Work," Lamberth Consulting, http://www.lamberthconsulting.com/about-racial-profiling/racial-profiling-doesnt-work.asp.

8. The United States is party to the UN Convention for the Elimination of All Forms of Racial Discrimination (CERD) and the International Convention on Civil and Political Rights (ICCPR), which clearly forbid racial profiling.

9. Most recently in an article written with Darrick Hamilton, an assistant professor at Milano The New School for Management and Urban Policy, "Race, Wealth, and Intergenerational Poverty," *American Prospect*, September 16, 2009.

10. Tamar Lewin, "Reed College's President Is Told to Crack Down on Campus Drug Use," *New York Times*, April 26, 2010, http://www.nytimes.com/2010/04/27/education/27reed.html.

11. See, e.g., William Stuntz, "Unequal Justice," *Harvard Law Review* 121 (June 2008): 1980–81, 2020–21.

12. Blacks make up 12 percent of the population, 14 percent of drug users, 33 percent of those arrested on drug charges, 46 percent of those convicted on drug charges, and 45 percent of those incarcerated on drug charges, as noted by Marc Mauer, executive director of the Sentencing Project, in his October 2009 testimony on racial disparities in the criminal justice system prepared for the House Judiciary Subcommittee on Crime, Terrorism, and Homeland Security.

13. Douglas Massey and LiErin Probasco, "Divergent Streams: Race-Gender Achievement Gaps at Selective Colleges and Universities," *Du Bois Review* 7, no. 1 (2010): 219–46.

14. To take the Implicit Association Test, go to https://implicit.harvard.edu. To better understand how the test works and your

results, go to https://implicit.harvard.edu/implicit/demo/faqs
.html.

15. Shankar Vedantam, "See No Bias," *Washington Post*, January 23, 2005, W12.

16. The order of the bias is highest among whites, then Asians, then Latinos, and lowest among blacks. Even though blacks deny the bias—and exhibit the lowest degree of bias—their IAT scores also show evidence of some bias. See, e.g., Mahzarin Banaji and Anthony Greenwald, *Mindbugs: The Science of Ordinary Bias* (New York: Random House, forthcoming).

17. Ibid. In the chapter "The Stealth of Stereotypes," Dr. Banaji and Dr. Greenwald analyzed the data from 85,742 race-weapon tests sampled at the Web site implicit.harvard.edu. She and her colleagues observed an extremely strong association of black faces and weapons "for all groups who took the test—white, Asian, Hispanic and even African Americans themselves." The size of the bias was largest in whites and Asians, next largest in Hispanics, and smallest in African Americans.

18. For an additional analysis of "racial literacy," please see Lani Guinier, "Race and Reality in a Front-Porch Encounter," *Chronicle of Higher Education*, July 30, 2009; Lani Guinier, "From Racial Liberalism to Racial Literacy: *Brown v. Board of Education* and the Interest-Divergence Dilemma," *Journal of American History* 91, no. 1 (June 2004): 92–118, available at http://www.law
.harvard.edu/faculty/guinier/publications/racial.pdf.

1

THE BILL OF RIGHTS FOR BLACK MEN

BRYONN BAIN

Bryonn Bain is a graduate of Harvard Law School and the founder of the Blackout Arts Collective. He has taught courses at New York University, Brooklyn College, Rikers Island Academy, and other universities and prisons, using the arts and popular culture to critically examine the prison crisis in America. He appeared on 60 Minutes *after his personal story of racial profiling was printed in the* Village Voice. *The multimedia stage production* Lyrics from Lockdown *(Official Selection, NYC Hip-Hop Theater Festival) weaves his story of wrongful imprisonment with the poetry and letters of death row survivor Nanon Williams through hip-hop, theater, spoken word, and song.*

In this piece, Bain describes being arrested, along with his brother and cousin, outside a nightclub in New York City

1

*in a case of mistaken identity. As Bain eloquently points out,
the only thing his identity had in common with that of the
actual perpetrators was the color of his skin.*

After hundreds of hours and thousands of pages of legal theory in law school, I finally had my first real lesson in the Law. While home in New York City from school for the weekend, I was arrested and held in a cell overnight for a crime that I witnessed someone else commit.

We left the Latin Quarter nightclub that night laughing that Red, my cousin, had finally found someone shorter than his five-foot-five frame to dance with him. My younger brother, K, was fiending for a turkey sandwich, so we all walked over to the bodega around the corner, just one block west of Broadway. We had no idea that class was about to be in session. The lesson for the day was that there is a special Bill of Rights for nonwhite people in the United States—one that applies with particular severity to black men. It has never been ratified by Congress because—in the hearts of those with the power to enforce it—the *Black Bill of Rights* is held to be self-evident.

As we left the store, armed only with sandwiches and Snapples, the three of us saw a group of young men standing around a car parked on the corner in front of the store. As music blasted from the wide-open doors of their car, the men appeared to be arguing with someone in an apartment above the store. The argument escalated when one of the young men began throwing bottles at the apartment window. Several other people who had just left the club, as well as a number of random passersby, witnessed the altercation and began scattering to avoid the raining shards of glass.

AMENDMENT I

CONGRESS CAN MAKE NO LAW ALTERING
THE ESTABLISHED FACT THAT A BLACK MAN IS A NIGGER.

My brother, cousin, and I abruptly began to walk up the street toward the subway to avoid the chaos that was unfolding. Another bottle was hurled. This time, the apartment window cracked, and more glass shattered onto the pavement. We were halfway up the block when we looked back at the guys who had been hanging outside the store. They had jumped in the car, turned off their music, and slammed the doors, and they were getting away from the scene as quickly as possible. As we continued to walk toward the subway, about six or seven bouncers came running down the street to see who had caused all the noise. "Where do you BOYS think you're going?!" yelled the biggest of this muscle-bound band of bullies in black shirts. They came after my family and me with outstretched arms to corral us back down the block. "To the 2 train," I answered. Just then, I remembered that there are constitutional restrictions on physically restraining people against their will. Common sense told me that the bouncers' authority couldn't possibly extend into the middle of the street around the corner from their club. "You have absolutely no authority to put your hands on any of us!" I insisted with a sense of newly found conviction. We kept going. This clearly pissed off the bouncers—especially the big, bald, white bouncer who seemed to be the head honcho.

AMENDMENT II

THE RIGHT OF ANY WHITE PERSON
TO APPREHEND A NIGGER WILL NOT BE INFRINGED.

The fact that the bouncers' efforts at intimidation were being disregarded by three young black men much smaller than they were only made matters worse for the bouncers' egos (each of us is under five-foot-ten and weighs no more than 180 pounds). The bouncer who appeared to be in charge warned us we would regret having ignored him. "You BOYS better stay right where you are!" barked the now-seething bouncer. I told my brother and cousin to ignore him. We were not in their club. In fact, we were among the many people dispersing from the site of the disturbance, which had occurred an entire block away from their "territory." They were clearly beyond their jurisdiction. Furthermore, the bouncers had not bothered to ask any of the many other witnesses what had happened before they attempted to apprehend us. They certainly had not asked us. A crime had been committed, and someone black was going to be apprehended—whether that black person was a crack addict, a corrections officer, a preacher, a professional entertainer, or a student at a prestigious law school.

Minutes after we had walked by the bouncers, I was staring at badge 1727. We were screamed at and shoved around by Officer Ronald Connelly and his cronies. "That's them, officer!" the head bouncer said, indicting us with a single sentence.

AMENDMENT III

NO NIGGER SHALL, AT ANY TIME, FAIL TO OBEY ANY PUBLIC AUTHORITY FIGURES—EVEN WHEN THOSE FIGURES ARE BEYOND THE JURISDICTION OF THEIR AUTHORITY.

"You boys out here throwin' bottles at people?!" shouted the officer. Asking any of the witnesses would have easily cleared up the issue of who had thrown the bottles, but the officer could not have cared less about that. My family and I were now being punished for the crime of thwarting the bouncers' unauthorized attempt to apprehend us. We were going to be guilty unless we could prove ourselves innocent.

AMENDMENT IV

THE FACT THAT A BLACK MAN IS A NIGGER IS SUFFICIENT PROBABLE CAUSE FOR HIM TO BE SEARCHED AND SEIZED.

Having failed to convince Connelly, the chubby, gray-haired officer in charge, of our innocence, we were up against the wall in a matter of minutes. Each of us had the legs of our dignity spread apart, was publicly frisked from shirt to socks, and then had our pockets rummaged through. All the while, Officer Connelly insisted that we shut up and keep facing the wall, or, as he told Red, he would treat us like we "were trying to fight back." Next, the officers searched through my backpack and seemed surprised to find my laptop and a law school casebook, which I had brought to the club so that I could get some studying done on the bus ride back to school.

We were shoved into the squad car in front of a crowd composed of friends and acquaintances who had been in the club with us and had by now learned of our situation. I tried with little success to play back the facts of the famous Miranda case in my mind. I was fairly certain these cops were in the wrong for failing to read us our rights.

AMENDMENT V
ANY NIGGER ACCUSED OF A CRIME IS TO BE PUNISHED WITHOUT ANY DUE PROCESS WHATSOEVER.

We were never told that we had a right to remain silent. We were never told that we had the right to an attorney. We were never informed that anything we said could and would be used against us in a court of law.

AMENDMENT VI

IN ALL PROSECUTIONS OF NIGGERS, THEIR ACCUSER SHALL ENJOY THE RIGHT OF A SPEEDY APPREHENSION, WHILE THE ACCUSED NIGGER SHALL ENJOY A DEHUMANIZING AND HUMILIATING ARREST.

After my mug shot was taken at the precinct, Officer Connelly chuckled to himself as he took a little blue-and-white pin out of my wallet. "This is too sharp for you to take into the cell. We can't have you slitting somebody's wrist in there!" he said facetiously. I was handed that pin the day before at the Metropolitan Museum of Art. I wanted to be transported back there, where I had seen the ancient Egyptian art exhibit that afternoon. The relics of each dynastic period pulled a proud grin across my face as I stood in awe at the magnificence of this enduring legacy of my black African ancestors.

This legacy has been denied for so long that my skin now signals to many that I must be at least an accomplice to any crime that occurs somewhere in the vicinity of my person. This legacy has been denied for so long that it was unfathomable to the cops that we were innocent bystanders in this situation. This legacy has been denied for so long that I lay locked up all night, for no good reason, in a filthy cell barely bigger than the bathroom in my tiny basement apartment in Cambridge, Massachusetts. This legacy is negated by the lily-white institutions where many blacks are trained to think that they are somehow different from the type of Negro this kind of thing happens to, because in their minds White Supremacy is essentially an ideology of the past.

Yet White Supremacy was alive and well enough to handcuff three innocent young men and bend them over the hood of a squad car with cops cackling on in front of the crowd, "These BOYS think they can come up here from Brooklyn, cause all kinds of trouble, and get away with it!"

AMENDMENT VII
NIGGERS MUST REMAIN WITHIN THE CONFINES
OF THEIR OWN NEIGHBORHOODS.
THOSE WHO DO NOT ARE CLEARLY LOOKING FOR TROUBLE.

Indeed, I had come from Brooklyn with my younger brother and cousin that evening to get our dance on at the Latin Quarter. However, having gone to college in the same neighborhood, I consider it to be more of a second home than a place where I can escape the eyes of my community and unleash the kind of juvenile mischief to which the officers were alluding. At twenty-five years old, after leaving college five years before and completing both a master's degree and my first year of law school, this kind of adolescent escapism was now far behind me. But that didn't matter.

The bouncers and the cops didn't give a damn who we were or what we were about. While doing our paperwork several hours later, another officer, who realized how absurd our ordeal was and treated us with the utmost respect, explained to us why he believed we had been arrested.

AMENDMENT VIII

WHEREVER NIGGERS ARE CAUSING TROUBLE,
ARRESTING ANY NIGGER AT THE SCENE OF THE CRIME
IS JUST AS GOOD AS ARRESTING THE ONE WHO IS ACTUALLY
GUILTY OF THE CRIME IN QUESTION.

After repeated incidents calling for police intervention during the last few months, the 24th Precinct and the

Latin Quarter had joined forces to help deal with the club's "less desirable element." To prevent the club from being shut down, they needed to set an example for potential wrongdoers. We were just unfortunate enough to be at the wrong place at the wrong time— and to fit the description of that "element." To make matters worse, from the bouncers' point of view, we had the audacity to demonstrate our understanding that for them to touch us without our consent constituted battery.

As Officer Connelly joked on about how this was the kind of thing that would keep us from ever going anywhere in life, the situation grew increasingly unbelievable. "You go to Harvard Law School?" he inquired with a sarcastic smirk. "You must be on a ball scholarship or somethin', huh?" I wanted to hit him upside his uninformed head with one of my casebooks. I wanted to water-board him with the sweat and tears that have fallen from my mother's face for the last twenty years, during which she has held down three nursing jobs to send six children to school. I wanted to tell everyone watching just how hard she has worked to give us more control over our own destinies than she had while growing up in her rural village in Trinidad. I still haven't told my mom what happened. Seeing the look on her face when I do will be the worst thing to come out of this experience. I can already hear the sound of her crying when she thinks to herself that none of her years of laboring in hospitals through sleepless nights mattered on this particular evening.

AMENDMENT IX

Niggers will never be treated like full citizens in America—no matter how hard they work to improve their circumstances.

It did not matter to the officers or the bouncers that my brother was going to graduate from Brooklyn College that June after working and going to school full time for the last six years. It did not matter that he had worked for the New Jersey Department of Corrections for almost a year. They didn't give a damn that I was the president of my class for each of the four years that I attended Columbia University. It did not matter that I was then in my second year at Harvard Law School. And in a fair and just society, none of that *should* matter. Our basic civil rights should be respected no matter who we are or the institutions with which we are affiliated. What should have mattered was that we were innocent. Officer Connelly checked all three of our licenses and found that none of us had ever been convicted of a crime.

AMENDMENT X
A NIGGER WHO HAS NO ARREST RECORD
JUST HASN'T BEEN CAUGHT YET.

It should have mattered that we had no record. But it didn't. What mattered was that we were black and we were there. That was enough for everyone involved to draw the conclusion that we were guilty until we could be proved innocent.

After our overnight crash course in the true criminal law of this country, I know from firsthand experience that the Bill of Rights for Black Men in America completely contradicts the one that was ratified for the society at large. The afternoon before we were arrested, I overheard an elderly white woman on the bus remark to the man beside her how much safer Mayor Giuliani has made New York City feel. I remember thinking to myself, "Not if you look like Diallo or Louima!"

It's about as safe as L.A. was for Rodney King, or as safe as Texas was for James Byrd Jr.; this list could go on for days. Although the Ku Klux Klan may feel safe enough to march in Manhattan, the rights of black men are increasingly violated every day by the New York City police and by police in other cities around the country. In the context of some of these atrocities, I suppose we were rather lucky to have been only abducted, degraded, pushed around, and publicly humiliated.

Addendum: After four court appearances over five months, the DA's case against Bryonn Bain, Kristofer Bain, and Kyle Vazquez was dismissed. No affidavits or other evidence were produced to support the charges against them.

2

REPORTING WHILE BLACK

SOLOMON MOORE

Solomon Moore was a criminal justice correspondent for the New York Times *based in Los Angeles from 2007 to 2010. His work focused on national law enforcement and crime trends, incarceration, and criminal justice policy. He covered the Iraq War from 2005 until 2008 for the* New York Times *and, before that, for the* Los Angeles Times. *He was a member of a four-person team in Baghdad that won a 2006 Overseas Press Club award. His bureau was also selected for an honorable mention for the Pulitzer Prize that year. In addition, he has worked in Africa, Israel and the Occupied Palestinian Territories, Egypt, Jordan, and Europe. He has two children.*

In his piece, Moore describes an encounter with the police in Salisbury, North Carolina, where he was reporting on

gang activity when he got caught up in the police depart-
ment's ongoing harassment of local youth.

He did not ask my name or my business. The police officer just grabbed my wrists, swung me around, and jerked my hands high behind my back. He levered me down onto the hood of his cruiser. My bald head made a distinct thump.

"You have no right to put your hands on me!" I exclaimed. "This is a high-crime area," said the tall white officer as he expertly handcuffed me. "You were loitering. We have ordinances against loitering."

In 2007, while talking to a group of young black men standing on a sidewalk in Salisbury, NC, for an article for the *New York Times* on the harsh anti-gang law enforcement tactics some law enforcement agencies use, I had discovered the main challenge to such measures: police have great difficulty determining who is, and who is not, a gangster—especially black gangsters.

I was not a gangster. I was a criminal justice reporter. I visited prisons and jails and detention centers. I pored through court records. I sat down with police chiefs and beat cops and federal agents and prosecutors. And I sought out pimps and drug dealers and gangsters to put them on the record.

My reporting was going well. I had gone to Salisbury to find someone with firsthand experience with North Carolina's tough anti-gang stance, and I had found that someone: me. Except, I didn't quite fit the description of the person I was seeking. I shared some common traits with the subjects of my reporting, but I wasn't really cut out for the thug life. At thirty-seven years old, I was already beyond my street-tough years. I suppose I could have been taken for an "O.G.," or "original gangster," except that I didn't roll like that—I drove a Volvo station wagon, paid a California mortgage, and had two young homeys in youth soccer leagues.

I should note that my racial identity is complex and fluid. My mother is a Jewish American immigrant raised in Chicago. My father is an African American descendent of slaves from the Piedmont region of South Carolina—further back than that, I can only speculate that his family originated somewhere in West Africa. I have ancestors that were Cherokee and Chickasaw. I imagine there are Irish immigrants in my family too, given my Irish surname and the number of textile mills and plantations that the Moores ran in the antebellum South. My family moved around a lot when I was a child. I have relatives of all persuasions and races, and my idiom is a jumble of the regional and ethnic accents I heard throughout my life.

I have also worked as a journalist in dozens of countries—I'd like to think that my travels have also shaped my identity, racial and otherwise. So has the experience of interviewing and writing about people from all walks of life. Sometimes I shift from one dialect to another depending on whom I am addressing. Sometimes I emphasize one aspect of my ethnic identity—my love of Jewish humor, my Midwestern directness, my Southern friendliness, my African American defiance—depending on my circumstances or my company. The mother of my children is a naturalized citizen, a Welsh-Polynesian American. I kid you not. My children are god knows what.

In other words, I am a typical American.

But of course, I am describing how I express my identity and how I experience it internally. Most Americans understand that identity—especially racial identity—is also shaped by outside forces: community, culture, politics, law, history. I do contain multitudes, but like many of my countrymen I am also a descendant of Jim Crow and an inheritor of the "one-drop rule," which makes me simply *black*.

I am black. I am African American. I don't mind Negro either. I experience this as well: an indivisible blackness. I am the benefactor of a redemptive culture born out of Africa, slavery, and an epic liberation movement that arcs from abolitionists and suffragists, to Civil War and Civil Rights. I lay claim to Prince and James Baldwin. I lay claim to Mahalia Jackson and Beyoncé; to Frederick Douglass, Allen Iverson, and Barack Obama.

But this wasn't the blackness I was living that night in Salisbury. That blackness was a different, clarifying blackness—the kind that reflects streetlamps on an indented police car hood. It was blackness with structure and historical weight. It was blackness undergirded by threat and by violence, and so defined and impenetrable that it almost seems invisible.

I had arrived in Salisbury around midnight, figuring that gang members would be more visible after dark, and found a local hangout with the help of a cabdriver. Striking up a conversation with young gang members in the middle of the night in an unfamiliar town is always a tricky proposition, even for a black man. But as a journalist, I have always counted on one common human trait I've witnessed and benefited from the world over: people want to tell their story, especially if they believe they're being victimized.

And I will say that blackness has its advantages for someone who does a lot of writing about minority communities. Blending in visually, sometimes cultur-ally, allows me to see things that others might miss. But even when my appearance has been helpful, those benefits rarely survive the first words out of my mouth, which usually signal—by accent or content—that I'm not from wherever I happen to be.

"What's the *New York Times* doing down here?" asked one man. His dreads overflowed a sock hat. He and about a dozen other black men stood in front of a clapboard house. I chose it because of the drug sales I observed while parked across the street. "Man, you a cop," said another man. "Hey, this guy's a cop!" "You've got me wrong," I said trying to sound casual. The men looked at me warily. I started to pull my press identification out of my wallet. "I'm a reporter. I'm just trying to talk to you about your neighborhood."

In the distance I heard neighborhood look-outs calling: "Five-O! Five-O!"—a universal code in American ghettos for the approaching police. I thought they were talking about me, but thought again as three police cars skidded to a stop in front of us. A tall white police officer got out of his car and ordered me toward him. Two other police officers, a white woman and a black man, stood outside of their cars nearby. I complied. Without so much as a question, the officer shoved my face down on the sheet metal and cuffed me so tightly that my fingertips tingled.

"They're on too tight!" I protested. "They're not meant for comfort," he replied. While it is true that I, like many of today's gang members, shave my head bald, in my case it's less about urban style and more about letting nature take its course. Undoubtedly, the young men watching me smooch the hood of the black-and-white had also been in this position—some of them, they would tell me later, with just as little provocation.

But here again I failed to live up to the "street cred" these forceful police officers had granted me. As the female officer delved into my back pocket for my wallet she found no cash from illicit corner sales, in fact no cash at all, though she did find evidence of my New York crew—my corporate identification card.

After a quick check for outstanding warrants, the handcuffs were unlocked and my wallet returned without apology or explanation beyond the suggestion that my approaching young black men on a public sidewalk was somehow flouting the law. "This is a dangerous area," one officer told me. "You can't just stand out here. We have ordinances."

"This is America," I said angrily. In that moment I was supremely unconcerned about whether this was standard police procedure, a useful law enforcement tool, or whatever anybody else wanted to call it. "I have a right to talk to anyone I like, wherever I like." The female officer trumped my naive soliloquy: "Sir, this is the South. We have different laws down here." I tried to appeal to the African American officer out of some sense of solidarity. "This is a bad area," he told me. "We have to protect ourselves out here."

As the police drove away, I turned again to my would-be interview subjects. Surely now they believed I was a reporter. I found their skepticism had only deepened. "Man, you know what would have happened to one of us if we talked to them that way?" said one disbelieving man as he walked away from me and my blank notebook. "We'd be in jail right now."

I look back on that night now and it all looks like a bad cliché. Cops swerving up to some random black man in the middle of the night and telling him they have different laws in the South while he's spread-eagled on the hood. Their casual references to a black neighborhood as a "bad area" governed by mysterious, and quite alien, ordinances now sound trite. Even my light defiance seems contrived to me on reflection; a bad Sidney Poitier impression.

I will admit now that I was never really concerned for my liberty or safety, even at midnight in North Carolina. I knew I was backed up by the law and by the resources of my employer. I already had a return ticket to California. I knew I could mouth off and pay no real consequence; I did, and it felt good. In fact, I knew I didn't fit the profile and that I was relatively safe, even in cuffs.

Of course, the police didn't know all of this, so there was a certain amount of danger in their approach. But what is instructive is that the police didn't fit the roles they were enacting, either. They acted and spoke like Jim Crow cops, but of course this is the twenty-first century. One officer was a woman, one was a black man, and the tall white officer turned out to be an immigrant from Europe. Just the way miscegenation laws did not envision, and tried mightily to thwart, the existence of someone like me, so too has our history spurned armed women, Negros with badges, and foreigners wearing uniforms on American soil.

And this is why racial profiling is so insidious. It creates encounters that exist outside time and identity. Regardless of who we all thought we were that night— a mixed-race *New York Times* reporter and three armed beneficiaries of the civil rights movement—our relationship immediately slid into a dreadful default position where the only critical matter at hand was the color of my skin. I see now that we were playing out a relationship that was not grounded in the reality of that moment; we were lip-synching to the echoes of a discredited past.

A couple of days before I visited Salisbury, I met with Patrick L. McCrory, the mayor of Charlotte, North Carolina. A white man, he was the longest-serving mayor in the city's history at the time and had become a lightning rod for racial tensions after his police department arrested 169 young men, most of them black, in downtown Charlotte during one night in 2007. Most of those men were eventually released without charges. He later retired in 2009 after an unsuccessful run for governor in 2008.

I asked the mayor about the charges of racial profiling leveled at him and the police. Mayor McCrory said that racial profiling had no place in policing, but he insisted that he had good information that 60 percent of all the city's gangsters were African American. Statistics like these are difficult to nail down. Who is a gangster? Someone who calls himself one? Whoever the police say is one? Whoever lives in a gang-infested neighborhood? And we know that most gangsters become inactive within two years, so are they counted too? How long is the half-life of the thug life?

The mayor himself acknowledged that policing can be imprecise, especially when it comes to rounding up gangsters: "This ganglike culture is tough to separate out. Whether that's fair or not, that's the truth," he told me.

Before I left, the mayor told me a story from his own life. He said he had taken in a black teenager and had hoped to turn his life around. The young man's father left him a long time ago, and his mother struggled to stay out of trouble. The mayor lamented that his charge had recently gotten a girlfriend pregnant and had been getting into trouble with the law. He wondered aloud whether anything short of God's grace or the criminal justice system could change the behavior of such wayward youths.

I wasn't sure what to make of the story when he told it. I wondered whether he was telling me a story to showcase his Christianity, or whether he was simply describing his common touch. When I reflect on it now, I think he was telling me that he sees black people as people and that his understanding of his city's population transcends racial profiling. The mayor also told me that by going after gangsters he was doing the bidding of many of his black constituents. I accept this. I don't think the mayor was racist.

I give those Salisbury officers the benefit of the doubt, too. I imagine they are not racists, either. But I happen to believe that racist acts do not always accompany racist intent or even racist thoughts. Racial profiling isn't racist because the people who designed these stop-and-frisk policies were racists; racial profiling is racist in its function. At root, it is a way of reinforcing racial identities we would not choose for ourselves—black men as suspects, as outlaws, as others. Racial profiling is racial categorization by state force.

That force—whether it be a five-minute detention, a baseless traffic stop, or a baton beating—changes us, the police officer, the suspect, and the country we all belong to. It warps us and impacts who we think we are and who we are to one another. Race-based policing can still be found in law and policy, but it is more ingrained than words on paper. Too many black men, including myself, have faced the same encounters too many times in too many places to conclude that racial profiling is simply a training problem or a legal issue plaguing scofflaw police agencies. Racial profiling is a cultural practice that arises from a power relationship that predates all of us. This is why it is so dangerous and persistent.

By the time I was sprawled out on the hood of the police cruiser, I had been stopped by the police many times. As a college student in the 1990s, I was pulled over three times in one week in South Carolina with my future wife in the car. That was always a wonder to her, but it is hard for me to avoid the conclusion that they stopped me because they saw a black boy riding around with a fair-skinned woman with flowing hair. I assume they didn't know she was from the tropics. I've been detained in my own predominately white Los Angeles neighborhood for looking like a robbery suspect. They assumed I did not live there, and I'm left to figure out why. I am routinely frisked at airports, and I find it hard to believe that I fit the profile of any terrorist I've ever heard about.

Law enforcement officials and their supporters usually avoid the term *racial profiling*, but they tell me they do believe in instincts and experience. Most police officers—especially those who work in urban areas—say that minorities make up a large share of their arrests because they commit the most crimes. This is simplistic at best. For instance, we know from surveys that white youths are just as likely (some say far more likely) to smoke marijuana than black youths, yet African Americans are more likely to be arrested for petty possession. Police make more arrests in neighborhoods where they decide to be present. That is why crime is so low on college campuses, for example, despite the existence of all kinds of behavior that would get kids in the projects in trouble. And that is why it concerns me when police officers identify "bad neighborhoods." Who gets to decide which neighborhoods are bad? What makes them bad?

Police officers have told me that it would be ridiculous to be blind to race or ethnicity. They say that years of police work give them an innate sense of who is within and without the law and what they look like. That might be true; I don't know. When police officers speak this way, it sounds to me like a defense of their way of seeing. More specifically, it seems like a defense of a particular way of seeing blackness. That way of seeing is unpredictable, and I am threatened by it. I think we all are.

And of course, we do see difference when we look at one another. We all make snap judgments based on physical appearance and the sound of voices. But just because these reactions are natural doesn't mean that they have any place in police work. We all categorize one another, but that doesn't mean we do so accurately or justly. And the way we see each other is often informed by our history together, or the lack thereof.

When I reported in Africa, people there quickly assumed I was a *mzungu*, or a white person, regardless of how I, or my country, thought of myself. In a way, they were right. I walked into some villages wearing clothes and gear that were worth more money than they would make in a year. Sometimes my "whiteness" was met with hostility; more unsettling were those occasions when I was granted unwarranted respect simply because of where I was born. But usually, to most of the rural Africans I met, my whiteness just meant I was foreign, an unknown. They had few preconceived notions of my identity because they had little to go on—a few Denzel Washington movies if they were lucky, Tupac on the radio, maybe. To them, my identity was mainly an empty space being filled by the accumulation of moments I shared with them. I was comfortable with that.

When I worked in Baghdad as a war correspondent, American soldiers at checkpoints leveled their guns at me on two occasions because they assumed I was an Iraqi and a possible threat. Both times, I avoided being shot by loudly identifying myself as an American. The soldiers (one of them African American) lowered their weapons after they heard my accent. I'm sure they assumed I was black, but out there—unlike in Salisbury—I was American. That said, I believe the practice of snap identifications based upon skin color and other physical characteristics has resulted in unnecessary humiliations and, in some cases, deaths in our two current wars.

The irony is that—despite the small number of journalists of color in this country—being an African American reporter has its advantages. In Third World nations, and especially in conflict zones, having some pigmentation can be a boon. I remember the difficulty a white colleague had in Rwanda when we were there covering the election of the current president, Paul Kagame, in 2003. When we visited the countryside, she could not walk around for five minutes without attracting a parade of a couple dozen children curiously following her. They barely noticed me, so I was able to do good work there. In Iraq, locals rarely assumed I was American since they associated U.S. citizens with camouflage, guns, or white skin. I had none of these, so I traveled all over the country and was rarely identified as a foreigner in public. I once walked through a throng of worshippers to pray in the glorious Shrine of Imam Ali in Najaf, Iraq, and I'm not even a Muslim.

That blackness the Salisbury officers imposed upon me never trammeled me during my travels. My blackness always feels more complex, more surprising, and more real outside America. I am always surprised—in a way that I was not surprised by those three officers—by how my blackness is perceived abroad.

I remember sitting down for an interview in a Baghdad mosque with a young Iraqi boy and his father suspected of having ties to the local Sunni Arab insurgency. The boy had been held and tortured over several days by Shiite policemen for no other reason than his religious sect. Although I had compiled a dossier of torture photos and first-person accounts of assassinations, I couldn't independently verify the boy's particular story because constant assaults on his neighborhood had rendered it inaccessible. So I interrogated the boy to make sure his story held up. With the help of a skilled interpreter, Shamil Aziz, I circled back to details the boy mentioned an hour or two earlier. I made him show the ligature marks on his wrists and the burn marks on his chest. I made him recount the beatings he had undergone over and over. He described the rooms he was locked in and the killings he witnessed. He told me how Shiite policemen took pity on his youth and released him.

His father brought his son to the mosque after I spent weeks negotiating with its clerics. These were hard-liners. The mosque often was involved in hostage negotiations between the United States and Sunni Arab guerrillas. It was a dangerous place, and we really shouldn't have stayed there so long. At the end of our interview, the father leaned across the table and told me that, as a Muslim, he was aware of the struggle of black Americans in my country. He told me he learned in school about black Muslims like Muhammad Ali and Malcolm X and that he admired them. He said that he learned from these men how black people were oppressed in the United States and that he therefore had compassion for me. It was a nationalist version of my blackness, a version I have long outgrown but that was still familiar to me.

And then he told me that he was offended by the manner in which I questioned his son, and that I had disrespected him and his son and angered him.

"And if you weren't black," he told me, glaring at me, "I would kill you right now."

3

THAT'S JOE MORGAN!

JOE MORGAN

Joe Morgan is a former Major League Baseball player; spending a majority of his career with the Cincinnati Reds, he also played for the Astros, Giants, and the Athletics. Morgan was the National League MVP in 1975 and 1976 and won the Gold Glove Award from 1972 to 1976. He was inducted into the Baseball Hall of Fame in 1990. Morgan is currently an Emmy-winning commentator for ESPN television and radio.

Morgan's Kafkaesque story of being detained by the LAPD at the Los Angeles airport speaks both to the indiscriminate nature of profiling and to the importance of efforts to seek justice and redress in the wake of such incidents.

In my first years with the Houston Astros, we had a game in San Francisco that was going to be nationally televised on NBC. The NBC announcers that day were Jackie Robinson and Pee Wee Reese. Though there were far more black players in the game than there had been a decade before, it was still a special thrill to see Jackie Robinson. In fact, I was approached before the game by the NBC staff and asked if I would consent to be interviewed. I agreed, realizing that the interviewer might be Robinson. I waited nervously in the dugout, not knowing what I might say, but hoping that Jackie, not Pee Wee, would be the interviewer. Then I saw Pee Wee walk over from the other dugout with his mike. So after the interview, I walked over to Jackie anyway. I introduced myself, as nervous and as awestruck as any rookie. I did not know what to say, other than wanting to convey to him in some way the debt of gratitude I owed him. He was a large man, larger than I realized from the many pictures I had seen of him. He was heavier and also older-looking than his years. His hair was prematurely white. I didn't know it, but he already was battling the major health problems that eventually shortened his life.

"Thank you" was all I could get out of my mouth.

Robinson smiled. His eyes, ever so slightly, seemed to brighten for a second. Then I just walked off to do my business.

Young black players today come into the game taking too much for granted. Because they can come and go, stay in the same hotels and eat in the same restaurants with their white teammates, they really have little sense of what it was like just a few decades ago—when Jackie Robinson broke in. As the song goes: "A people without knowledge of their history is like a tree without roots."

I left the office one afternoon in March of 1988 to catch a flight to Tucson for an LPGA celebrity golf tournament. I used to go there every year to help raise money for charity. I left Oakland at about 4:30 in the afternoon and had to change planes in L.A. When I got off at LAX and walked from one gate to the other, it was announced that the plane I needed to catch was delayed. So I sat around in the lounge area talking to people, signing autographs. All of this was very friendly and cordial. Perfect strangers, who knew me from TV, told me how much they liked my baseball telecasts. And then some guy came over and said that the delay was going to be longer than anticipated. I excused myself because I needed to go and call ahead to Tucson to let them know that I was going to arrive late. I went to the phone booth just beyond the lounge area, leaving my bags right where they were.

As I was dialing my number, a guy put his hand on my shoulder and forcefully whirled me around.

"Hey, what's your problem?" I said, looking into a hard, hostile face.

Without identifying himself, he said: "We've got the guy you're traveling with, and you're coming with me."

"I don't know what you're talking about," I said. "I just got off the plane, I'm not with anyone."

"You're coming with me," he said.

"I don't want to go with you. I haven't done anything."

He said, "You have identification?"

I told him that I did, and I turned to start walking back to my bags. Before I could take a step, he grabbed me.

"Hey, what's your problem, man? Let me get my bag and I'll identify myself." The guy had never asked who I was and didn't seem interested in finding out now. Just then, one of the people in the lounge area who happened to be at the next phone tried to intercede.

"That's Joe Morgan, the broadcaster, the baseball star," he said. "I was on the plane with him from Oakland."

"Get the fuck away from here or I'll take you in with him!" the guy said. My witness left.

By this time, I was getting a little shaky because it was slowly dawning on me that there was nothing I could do to identify myself or save myself from what was going to happen.

"Okay," I said, "what do you want me to do?"

He pointed over my right shoulder, indicating that he wanted me to go that way. When I turned, he pinned my arms behind me, put his knee in my back, and knocked me to the ground.

"Why are you doing this to me?" I cried out. I couldn't think of anything else to say.

"I'm an authority figure. I'll show you what authority is; you've been up against us before." I did not know what he meant then or now. I thought he was crazy.

When this cop's partner walked up, he said to him, "D'you see him take a swing at me?"

The other cop said, "Yes."

Over the next hours, the nightmare deepened, and it was all because I was just another black man. No longer protected by celebrity, as anonymous as any other black man, I was exposed to whatever undeserved fury was going to be meted out.

I was cuffed, taken into custody, and held for some time in a security area of the airport. Here, there were no witnesses, and no one to stand up for me. Anything could happen, I realized. Finally, a woman walked in, perhaps an official of some kind, who seemed to recognize me. She left, the two cops huddled for a while, and then the arresting cop came over to me and said, "Well, maybe you're who you say you are."

I wanted to say, "I never told you who I was; I never had the chance," but instead, I just kept quiet. In no way did I want to be provocative. He said, "If I let you go, you promise to forget about this?" I didn't immediately answer because I wasn't about to forget it. He repeated his offer. This time I said, "You do what you have to do, and I'll do what I have to do."

"Tell you what," this bright light said, "I think I'll call the newspapers and tell them we're holding Joe Morgan on a drug investigation. How do you think that'll play?" I said nothing. After another standoff, the cop looked at his partner and between them they decided to take the cuffs off and let me go.

As soon as I was out of there, I went to airport security and told them what had happened. They told me their people weren't involved, that it was the LAPD. Learning that, I went to the nearest LAPD substation and tried to file a formal complaint.

The night was by no means over. I was not allowed to file a complaint. As I was in the process of requesting information on how to file, the two cops who roughed me up turned up again and began screaming at me. I felt lucky just to get out of there. This incident happened without any press fanfare.

Because I had been unable to file a complaint, I filed a lawsuit against the LAPD. But in no way did that change my sense that the struggle begun by such pioneers as Jackie Robinson still remains only a promise. The reality, far more deadly, is that too many people, black and white, have simply settled into newer, safer forms of the old thinking. It is therefore doubly painful to me to see young people, especially young black people, without any real memory of the past.

Some might counter that I have nothing to complain about—that I have achieved worldly success far beyond what most white people in this country achieve. That is, as my experience in Los Angeles showed, quite beside the point. Charles Barkley, the basketball star, raised a lot of eyebrows when he told a roomful of media people that, although he was habitually treated with smiles, friendliness, and respect, the real question was how an anonymous black person would be treated by the same people. Charles is usually outspoken, but his words often hit the mark. This time, he was a little off. I'm a celebrity, and that didn't help me a bit.

Addendum: Joe Morgan's lawsuit convinced the trial judge that the police had violated his rights. In reviewing the case, the appellate court compared the testimony from Morgan and the police officers, as well as the eyewitness account of the bystander. This comparison provides a rare official look at the different perspectives on profiling: what the police often say to justify their actions versus how the people profiled describe their experience.

What follows is how the appellate court recounted the evidence.

A. JOE MORGAN'S TESTIMONY

On March 15, 1988, Joe Morgan was at LAX waiting for a flight to Phoenix. He passed the time in the gate area, chatting with people who recognized him. At some point during his layover, he decided to make a phone call. Leaving his bags at the waiting area, he headed to some phone banks about forty feet away. According to Morgan, while he was dialing, [LAPD] Agent Searle grabbed his shoulder and turned him around. Morgan asked Searle what he wanted. Searle insisted that Morgan was traveling with another person. Morgan responded that he was traveling alone, and asked again what the problem was. According to Morgan, Searle responded with words to the effect of "I'm doing a drug investigation and you're a part of it." Morgan again said he was alone; Searle insisted that Morgan was "with this guy" and told him "you are coming with me." Morgan replied, "Why am I coming with you? I didn't do anything. I am making a phone call." Searle did not tell Morgan that he was free to go.

Searle asked Morgan for identification. Morgan replied that it was in his luggage, approximately forty feet away. Morgan took a step toward his luggage, and Searle grabbed his upper torso and told him, "I will put you on the ground if you don't come with me." Morgan testified that after this exchange, a bystander came up and said to the effect, "That's Joe Morgan, the baseball player, and I can identify him." Searle responded with hostility, flashing his identification and warning the bystander to back off.

Morgan testified that at that moment he began to get frightened: "Well, at that point . . . I became very nervous. Before that, you know, I was standing up, kind of saying, 'Hey, I don't want to go with you. Let me get my ID' or whatever, but he was very hostile. . . . I felt like it didn't matter if I did have my ID. . . . He was going to do something to me. . . . I said to him, 'Okay. Where do you want me to go?'" According to Morgan, Searle responded by pointing over Morgan's shoulder. As Morgan turned toward that direction, Searle grabbed him around the neck from behind, forced Morgan to the floor, and handcuffed him.

While Morgan was on the ground, [LAPD] Agent Woessner came up with another man, Tony Floyd. As

Woessner approached, Searle asked him, "You saw him swing at me, didn't you?" According to Morgan, one of the officers asked Floyd if Morgan "was the guy that was with you?" and Floyd answered no.

Searle pulled Morgan to his feet, and led him down the concourse, past the waiting area where Morgan had just been signing autographs. As they passed Morgan's luggage, Morgan again asked to be allowed to get his identification. Searle placed his hand over Morgan's mouth and nose and led him into a small room marked "nursery." Morgan testified that he had difficulty breathing and felt totally out of control. *Inside the nursery room, Floyd repeated that Morgan was not the person he was with.* Morgan testified that Searle threatened to report to the press that he was a part of a narcotics investigation and offered to release Morgan if Morgan would promise to forget what had happened. Morgan responded, "You do what you have to do, and I'll do what I have to do." After a few moments of further exchange, Searle removed the handcuffs and allowed Morgan to leave.

According to Morgan, at no time during this course of events did he make any aggressive or hostile physical gestures toward either Searle or Woessner. He testified that at no time did he resist, use profanity, or scream.

B. RICHARD RUYBALID'S TESTIMONY

Richard Ruybalid, an individual not otherwise associated with Morgan, was on the same plane into LAX as Morgan and was waiting for the same connecting flight to Phoenix. Ruybalid had recognized Morgan on the flight, but did not speak to him. Ruybalid testified that he was making a call from the same phone bank as Morgan when Searle approached Morgan. Ruybalid's attention was caught by a "heated conversation." Ruybalid approached to within ten feet, and witnessed the confrontation between Morgan and Searle. Ruybalid heard Searle saying to Morgan, "Come along. Come with us. Come with us." Morgan responded, "No, I am not going. Leave me alone. I want to get my identification." According to Ruybalid, Searle was insistent, repeating, "You are coming with us. Forget it. You are coming with us right now."

Ruybalid moved in closer and said, "Hey, what are you doing? That's Joe Morgan the famous baseball player." Searle responded by flashing his ID and saying, "Back off; narcotics officer." Ruybalid testified that at this time Morgan was not doing anything threatening or violent, but that Morgan's demeanor was defensive, bothered, angry. Ruybalid testified that Searle was very angry and his tone of voice very stern, and that Ruybalid felt he was being ordered to leave the area by a person of authority.

Ruybalid backed away, but continued to monitor the situation, remaining within fifteen or twenty feet from Morgan and Searle. He did not see Morgan taken to the floor, but he heard the noise caused by that fall. He testified that prior to that noise, he did not hear any yelling, screaming, or swearing. When he heard the noise of the fall, Ruybalid approached the men; he observed Searle pull Morgan to his feet and lead him away, holding his hand over Morgan's mouth. Ruybalid testified that Morgan walked reluctantly but did not resist, and that he did not use any profanity or scream.

C. DEFENDANTS' TESTIMONY

On March 15, 1988, Searle and Woessner were on a routine narcotics patrol at LAX. They observed Tony Floyd, a black man, moving rapidly through the concourse. Floyd had a carry-on bag which appeared to be half-empty. Floyd made eye contact with Searle and Woessner, and then looked away. To the agents, he appeared to be nervous. Finding these actions suggestive of narcotics involvement, Searle and Woessner decided to question Floyd.

Searle and Woessner identified themselves to Floyd and told Floyd that he was not under arrest and that he was free to go. Floyd agreed to talk with them. They asked him for identification, but he had none. They asked to look at his ticket, and he produced a one-way cash ticket issued in a name other than Floyd. They obtained permission to search his person and his carry-on bag; they found only clothing and toiletries. They then took Floyd to the men's room and conducted a pat down search which revealed nothing illegal, but did reveal that Floyd was carrying a second ticket. Although Floyd initially claimed to be traveling alone, he eventually admitted that he had a travel companion. Floyd did not remember the second person's name, but told the agents that the second traveler should be right behind him. The agents asked Floyd what the traveler looked like; Floyd responded, "He looks like me."

Based on their exchange with Floyd, the agents concluded that Floyd was a drug courier and that his companion was the "mule," the person who actually carried the drugs. The officers handcuffed Floyd, and left the bathroom with him to look for the second traveler. As they stepped out, they observed Morgan walking in their direction. The officers testified that Morgan was not running or dressed unusually. The only thing that linked Morgan to Floyd was that both men were black. The officers found this significant because Floyd had said that the second traveler looked like him, and in their experience couriers tended to work with people of their own ethnic group. According to Searle and Woessner, when Morgan got within twenty feet of the trio he looked directly at them, stopped, and then abruptly turned around and started walking in the direction from which he had come.

Searle followed Morgan, and approached him as he was standing facing a telephone with the receiver in his hand. According to Searle, he tapped Morgan on the shoulder, displayed his identification card, and said, "I'm a police officer." Morgan immediately replied, "I don't give a fuck who you are." When Searle asked for identification, Morgan responded by saying, "I don't have to show you shit. I don't have any identification." Searle told Morgan that he was conducting a narcotics investigation and that he wanted to determine if Morgan was traveling with anyone. Morgan responded by stating that he hadn't done anything and by repeatedly yelling at increasing volume, "You're not a police officer." Searle stated that he handed his police identification to Morgan, and that Morgan examined it and handed it back.

At that point, Searle testified that a citizen stepped forward, but that he did not remember him offering to identify Morgan. Searle testified only that he showed Ruybalid his ID and told him that he was a police officer.

Searle then told Morgan that he wanted Morgan to go with him to see if he was traveling with somebody, and Searle gestured toward the direction of Agent Woessner. Searle testified that he did not believe Morgan was free to go at that moment and that he believed that Morgan was required to show him some identification. Morgan kept asking "Why? Why?" and Searle repeated his request:

Searle: I kept explaining to him that I wanted to see if he was traveling with somebody, and eventually he starts walking with me. We probably take about three or four steps before he freaks out, before he starts screaming and then yelling.

Question: Okay. So you said, "I want to take you to some location or to take you to somebody so they can identify you?"

Searle: I said, "I'd like you to go with me to see if you're traveling with this person we're investigating. That's all I want to do. I want to see if you are together and then we can solve this," and he's screaming "Why? Why?" at the top of his lungs, but then he starts walking with me. I'd take a step, and he'd take a step with me, and we eventually take some steps toward where I last left Agent Woessner and Mr. Floyd.

Question: So at this point, you were starting to leave the area of the phone bank?

Searle: Yes, we did.

Question: Okay. And about how far were you from the phone bank when you stopped again?

Searle: Probably maybe got 10 feet away eventually.

Searle and Morgan walked toward Woessner and Floyd. According to Searle, after a few moments Morgan "freaked out" and began gesturing wildly, screaming at the top of his lungs. Woessner testified that he could hear Morgan yelling from some distance. Both officers testified that Morgan was waving his arms wildly; Searle had to duck to avoid getting hit and was bumped by Morgan's body. Searle grabbed Morgan around the chest and they fell to the floor; Searle ended up on top of Morgan. Searle testified that he told Morgan to put his hands behind his back, and that Morgan cooperated. Searle then got handcuffs from Woessner and cuffed Morgan.

Searle testified that then Morgan began screaming "Help! Help!" at the top of his lungs. As they walked down the concourse, Searle testified that he put his hand over Morgan's mouth to shut him up, because he was afraid that Morgan's screaming would attract attention and "he didn't want another fight to break out with somebody else jumping in because he's screaming." Searle did not inform Morgan that he was under arrest or read him his rights. Once in the nursery room, Searle released Morgan after Floyd verified that Morgan was not his companion.

*　　*　　*

Instructed by the trial judge that the police had violated Morgan's rights, the jury awarded him more than $500,000 in damages. For its part, the appellate court concluded:

> There is no claim that Morgan was dressed in an unusual manner, that he was hurrying through the airport, that he was carrying anything unusual, that he seemed nervous, or that any of the other factors normally relied upon in justifying investigatory stops at airports existed. [. . .] Accordingly, we agree with the district court that no reasonable suspicion justified the seizure of Morgan.

4

ON THE CORNER

RICHARD F.

Richard F. is nineteen years old and was born and raised in East Harlem. He recently graduated from Washington Irving High School in Manhattan. He is looking for a job, and is also considering continuing his education. He likes to spend time with family and friends and enjoys traveling to North Carolina to visit relatives.

In his account of a series of encounters with the police, Richard illustrates the consequences of arbitrary, ongoing stop-and-frisk policies: young people who "really don't trust" the police and wouldn't think to call them "if they got robbed walking down the street."

ON THE CORNER . . .

"**M**ove. Move off this corner." You're not sup-posed to be on the corner. I might be hav-ing a conversation with my friends or just hanging out for a little bit. Sometimes they say, "please move," but other times they curse at us. Or they threaten us and say, "Get the f-outta here. Get the f-outta here before I arrest you." It's like I'm doing something wrong when I'm not. It happens to all of my friends. We all chill to-gether and they just bother us all the time. They don't bother the grown people as much as they bother us teens. They just come straight to us. I don't get wild with them. I might say, "Come on. We just got here." But then I leave. I can't stand there because I know I'm going to get arrested. They've even pushed me before. We get screamed at by cops for no reason. They feel like they can do whatever and just keep on walking.

Where I live, a lot of police and DTs [detectives] hop out on people to search them and see if they got a gun on them. DTs are the worst; I never argue with them. You can tell DTs by their uniform, or sometimes by their car. In the hood, if there's a gray Impala, then you know it's the boys. I don't see them hop out on grown adults as much as they hop out on teens. It happens all the time where I live. They hop out and say, "What you got?" Then they get right back in their car. Sometimes they just search pockets, take money from us, and just go right back in their car. I've definitely seen that happen. One time, I saw a detective stop a guy and search him. He found weed on him and just took it. Didn't arrest him, just took his weed and left him alone. Another time they stopped my man John. They took his watch and his chain and just drove off.

You can't even pass money around. Say my friend wants to give me a dollar. That's seen as a drug transaction. Once, I went to the store at like three o'clock in the morning. I see my best friend; he had just come from the store. He passed me a dollar. He went the other way, and I was going to the store. I told him I was going to meet him in the house. A DT stopped him, but I didn't even know that was happening at the time. Then another one started running after me and checking me. I said, "Yo, what happened? What's going on?" He didn't say anything at all, just started running after me for no reason. He had on a black hoodie, and I felt like I should have just ran because I didn't know if someone was trying to stick me up or what. He didn't have a badge on or anything, so normally I could've thought someone was chasing me. But I knew it was a cop because it was a fat Caucasian guy.

AT HOME . . .

I go inside my building and the police think I have something [drugs, weapons] on me. But I don't. I respectfully tell them I don't. But they still check me. They check me in places I feel like they are not supposed to check, like up the inside of my leg. I tell them, "Excuse me. Watch out for my area," but they just do it anyway. If I ask them why they are searching me, they just make up a reason. They lie. Let's say I have on a red sweater. They might say someone with a red sweater was reported for doing something—a lie so that they can search me or my friends. I know that it isn't legal for them to search me for no reason, but they can just say I look suspicious. I've tried to speak up and tell them they can't search me, but they say they don't care. So I just let them. What's the point? If I try to argue with them, there are going to be more cops coming. For questioning what they say, there will be a whole pile of cops in my building, just for me.

THE COPS . . .

Sometimes I think cops go wild because a lot of teens are going wild themselves. I don't like it here in New York anymore. I want to leave and move to North Carolina, where my father and brother live. It seems like every day you hear about somebody getting shot and killed [in New York]. I'm always hearing that something happened on the East Side. It's like everybody's just dying . . . it's hard. With everybody going wild, there's a lot of stuff you can't handle sometimes. There's murderers and killers out there. If there's something big going on, we need cops for that. We don't have anyone else to ask. But even though it's good to have cops, I wouldn't call them. Maybe if they were to change certain things, like how they act in the community, they'd be good. But as it is, I don't like the police. I really don't trust them at all. If I got robbed walking down the street, I would never think to call the police. That would be like snitching. The way I see it, being a cop is like putting everybody down. Most times I just try to stay upstairs in my building. I try to stay in the house. I just don't come out.

Police are bothering everyone, whether they

commit a crime or not. Normally, you see so many cops as soon as you get into my projects. But let's say something happens—a fight breaks out on the block or somebody starts shooting—then it seems like you don't see any cops around. Everybody is doing bad and good. There are some dirty cops out there, and there are people that deal with the cops, all doing bad and good. But it's like they point towards the fact that some are doing bad, and then everybody is getting arrested for no reason. Cops need to change their act. They need to stop harassing us. If they were nice to us, we would be nice to them. We want respect, but they treat us all the same.

5

JUST-US

THE HONORABLE DANIEL K. DAVIS

Since 1997, Daniel K. Davis has been a Democratic member of the U.S. House of Representatives, representing Illinois' Seventh Congressional District. He has launched several successful campaigns to improve the quality of life for others, including the passage of the Second Chance Bill, which gives ex-offenders the opportunity to become productive citizens. Despite a 1991 run for mayor of Chicago, he is primarily interested in national issues, especially those related to ex-offenders, reentry, and other issues affecting African American males.

When Davis was stopped by police while driving home from hosting his weekly Sunday night radio show, he took his case to court, using an instance of racial profiling as an opportunity to educate and to "convince people that making use of the judicial system makes good sense."

I was on my way home from a radio show that I do every Sunday evening from 10 to 12. It's a free-wheeling general politics show where we talk about everything, taped in Chicago at the old WVON station on the South Side. I had three people in the car whom I was driving home and who had been guests on the show. One was a fellow who was an ex-offender, had been in prison for nine and a half years, and had managed to go through a training program (that was actually named after me). He had gotten a job making $22 an hour and had just been offered a job for $65,000 a year. We were all excited about having him, his wife, and the fellow who ran the training program on the show.

There were four of us in the car. I'm an aging African American male with gray hair and a gray beard, and on this night, I probably had on a suit and a tie. We were in a black sedan—a normal car, nothing fancy about it, nothing that would draw attention. The other three people were probably around forty years old. We didn't look like any bad actors. We were just driving along, feeling good. I was coming north on Kedzie Avenue, as I do every week. Nothing else was on the street except us. It was a little after twelve o'clock.

We looked up, and there was a police car behind us, lights flashing, but no siren. The officer got out of his car, came over to ours, and asked if I had a driver's license. I said that I did. He then asked if I had an insurance card. I indicated that I did. I pulled it out and gave it to him. As he was giving me my insurance card back, I said to him, "Well, you know, I'm on my way home, and I'm going to drop these people off. I'm just finishing up my radio show." I politely asked him, "Could you tell me why you stopped me?" And for a moment he didn't seem to have a reason. He seemed to take offense. It was as if he was asking, "Who are you to question and ask me why?" He didn't actually say that, but I could infer it from his voice and his demeanor. I didn't ask him in a haughty way; I just asked him in a very pleasant way, "Why did you stop me?"

He eventually said, "I noticed you weaving back there."

"Weaving? You've got to be joking, mistaken. I didn't weave."

"You were driving left of center," the officer said.

"Left of center? What is that?"

"Well, you went across the yellow line."

"Oh, you've just got to be mistaken." I knew I

couldn't have been driving left of center. At one point, there was a truck in front of me making a left turn, and I had gone to the right in order to go around the truck.

"Well, I'm going to give you a ticket," said the officer.

"Give me a ticket? For what?"

"For driving left of center."

"I just don't understand this." I looked at the other people in the car and asked, "Did you all observe me driving left of anything?"

I drive pretty normally; I don't even drive fast. I'm pretty conscientious. I don't speed, I don't drink on Sundays (I hardly drink at all), and the only medication I take is in the morning for diabetes. On hearing about this incident, I had people who've ridden with me call and say they were totally shocked. I'm a pretty solid, law-abiding, civic-minded, Christian-minded, good-guy citizen. I think we were stopped because it was after twelve o'clock at night, there were four black people in a car, and somebody just made a decision: let's stop these people. There was nothing else that I could point to. We were observing all traffic laws.

And so we had a little bit of an altercation. I said, "Well, do what you got to do." I just knew that I could go talk to someone reasonable. We weren't far from the police station. After he gave me the ticket (and took my driver's license), I went over to the station and asked to see the watch commander. But the watch commander was conducting roll call and was tied up, or so they said. I ended up speaking with the sergeant, who offered to call the officers to see if they could come in and adjudicate this and get it over with.

They came in and just simply refused. "They want the ticket to stand, and we can't overrule them or anything," said the sergeant. "It sounds like you were telling the truth, but you know, I can't overrule."

"OK, well, thank you very much," I said.

"Well, you know, I'll give you a bond, and you can keep your driver's license."

So I went home to bed. And the next day, of course, I called the Office of Professional Standards—well, they've changed the name—and shared with them what had happened. It was not so much about Danny Davis, the congressman, but mostly about the fact that this happens far too often to citizens. Every time there's an infraction, it doesn't necessarily mean that someone gets beat across the head with a billy club, or somebody pulls his gun and shoots. But many African Americans feel what's going on is criminal. I stopped in a restaurant a few days afterward and everybody there had a story about having been stopped unjustifiably by the police at some point during his lifetime.

The very next night after I got the ticket, I went to a meeting that a group of ministers had called because there had been a police shooting in the neighborhood. The police had shot a person and killed him. The people were attacking the ministers. Another friend of mine who is a state senator was there, and they started criticizing us for being impotent. They said the police just beat up on them and harass them and get away with it; nothing happens. They said, "you guys don't understand this the way we do because they don't treat you the same way they treat us." So when it came my time to speak, I told them my story of what had happened just the night before, in order to say, "we understand because we go through the same thing that you go through."

A reporter was present and wrote a story about it for the *Chicago Daily Defender*, a black views newspaper. I got a call from former judge Eugene Pincham:

"I heard you had a run-in with the police. Do you have a lawyer?"

"Well, judge, I don't have one yet."

"Well, you've got one now."

Of course, Gene Pincham is a renowned guy—I mean, super renowned. Unfortunately, he died the day that we were to go to trial. He had been diagnosed with cancer. I had to get another lawyer, and I didn't pay the $75 ticket. I want to believe that, as a citizen in this country, I have equal protection under the law, that I can have a situation assessed fairly, and that a court of law can determine the proper outcome. I think I was wrongfully stopped, and certainly I think I was wrongfully given a citation. So I went to court, and of course there was a continuance.*

Ultimately, after I had gone to court, I received a plea offer that this could go away permanently and that they would reduce the charges. I said I couldn't do that. Why would I do that? That would be admitting to something that never happened. We went to

---

*A continuance is a postponement of a date of a trial, hearing, or other court appearance to a later fixed date by order of the court, or upon a legal agreement by the attorneys and approved by the court.

court two or three times, and then the judge had a trial. The interesting thing was that the officer who wrote the ticket and did all of the interacting was not there; he never appeared in court. My lawyer raised the issue with the judge, who said either one of the officers could appear. When we finally got around to the trial, the female officer who had been there at the time appeared, not the male officer who did the talking. I couldn't believe it when she gave her side of the story. She said that I was in a gray car, but I had a black car. She also said I had made a left turn off a street that I'd never been on. The judge listened and said it just didn't sound like it happened.

This incident occurred in 2007, and at that time, I kind of blew up a little bit. But in reality, this has been happening all of my life. Over the years, I have been stopped by the Chicago police so many times I couldn't count them. I've always lived in inner-city Chicago. When I was younger, during the '60s, I had a full beard, which I wore kind of natural, like a lot of folks, and I often wore dashikis. I drove an old car for a long time, and I just would get stopped. We'd go through the driver's license check, car search kind of deal. They would say things like, "Well, you're driving an old car." I remember one guy told me I fit a profile, and I said, "Profile?" He said, "Yeah, you know, you just fit." The same thing continued to happen after I got elected to the City Council. I felt that I was stopped for driving while being black.

In many instances, the average citizen would not have been in a position to pursue this all the way through or would not have taken the time to do it. I have always tried to convince people that making use of the judicial system makes good sense. And of course, there are many people who don't have much faith in the judicial system, and therefore they do not use it nearly as effectively as they could. And I didn't want to be guilty of that.

In many locations throughout the country, you go to traffic court and you can spell justice—J-U-S-T dash U-S—just us. So black people don't know how to drive? We don't know how to observe traffic laws? Is there some difference between our approach to driving an automobile and the approaches that other people use? I find that pretty difficult to believe. If people feel that they can do things and get away with them—that there are no consequences, or it's accepted because it's in a certain community or neighborhood or because it was done to certain kinds of people—then of course it continues. But when something checkmates the situation, it reduces the likelihood of continuation or perpetuation. If we made greater use of the judicial system, we would get more results.

I already know that justice is a hard-won thing and that each generation has to win it and win it again. Laws are a big help, but there has to be something beyond the presence of law. Change requires, sometimes, a certain amount of sacrifice. And, if we're not willing to sacrifice, then we're not going to get the results that we are looking for. When I was in court, a number of young men came over to me afterward and said, "We really are glad that you went all the way through with this, because this happens to us all the time."

6

CHIPPED AWAY

NII-ODOI GLOVER

Nii-Odoi Glover is father to daughter Naa-Odoley. He attended school in Washington, D.C., and for the past few years he has been based in Los Angeles, California, where he works in event marketing, although he plans to relocate back to Washington, D.C., soon. His account of being accosted by the police while driving his car, walking down the street, and watching his daughter on the playground illustrates the pernicious and cumulative effects of feeling not like "a protected citizen, but rather that citizens were to be protected from me." "Who knows," Glover pointedly asks, "how these experiences will tally up in my psyche?"

My experiences with the police started off when I was a teenager in Washington, D.C. Just walking down the street, in what was then commonly known as "Chocolate City," the cops would stop me and my friends and verbally harass us about where we were going and what we were doing—all under the pretense that they were "looking for someone that fits your description." This was the socialization that we went through. Even though we came from diverse backgrounds, were of various ages, and had various levels of education, we were all stopped and harassed regularly by the cops.

By my mid-twenties, I had dreadlocks, which seemed to increase the harassment. I got stopped at least once a month, sometimes three times a month. My roommate at the time was aware of the situation and understood that if he was to ride anywhere with me, we had to plan to leave early enough to account for the time spent if we were to be stopped. We would try to make a joke out of it: "Here come your boys!" he would say when cops behind us would turn on their sirens.

As I got a little bit older, I started working in the mailroom at Georgetown University. At the time, the mail sorting facility was located in Virginia, which meant that I had to make the daily drive across the river. From the time I was a little kid, I always was told to watch myself even more when driving in Virginia with its state troopers. My peers would caution me to make sure all my papers were in order in the car and not to have anything even resembling an illegal substance in the car. The old heads in the community would tell us stories about how Virginia has a history of abuse against blacks and about how they were told by their own elders about the long train of abuses against blacks, dating back to slavery. I heard story after story about black men being caught with only a joint of marijuana and serving five to ten years for "intent to distribute." The stories may have been exaggerated, but the point was clear: Virginia was not to be taken lightly.

After leaving work one day, I was stopped before I got back into D.C. I was told that I had not used a turn signal. I'm not sure whether I did or not, but I knew the routine—there was always some arbitrary law that you may or may not have broken that is used as an excuse to verify your license and run your information to check for warrants. I have heard that cops think they have a "50/50" chance if they stop a black guy—meaning half the time they'd get a black guy on some type of infraction or find a reason to lock him up. A black man is the "usual suspect."

So here I am, stopped by this cop in northern Virginia, and the cop plays the nice guy routine, asking me with a smile if he can search the car while his partner checked my license. Now, black men know, if they have any sense, that you should never let the police search your car without a warrant. A cop can plant anything he wants while he is in your car, and then it's your word against his.

So I tell the cop, "No. You can't search my car." At this point, other squad cars are pulling up and surrounding my car as if I'm going to suddenly dash off and lead them on a high-speed chase through the bumper-to-bumper rush-hour traffic. The officer then starts to prod me with inappropriate questions, such as, "Why can't we check your car?" "Do you have anything illegal in the car?" "Do you have any weapons?" "Are you sure you don't have anything?" "You must be hiding something. If you weren't hiding anything, you would let us check your car."

I remained silent because I was starting to feel annoyed and disrespected. I'd had a long day of work at a job that lets me pay the bills and allows me to pay my taxes—the taxes that are supposed to secure my right to be protected, not harassed. The cop continued on with the line of questioning, and I continued to remain silent or spoke just enough to say "no" to his continued requests to search my car. His questions became more outrageous: "Hey man, are you sure you don't have any crack on you?"

"Is he serious?" I thought to myself. Finally, the officer gave me back my license and told me that I was free to go.

It's hard to explain how I felt. More than anything, I was just hurt. Here I am—a young father and hardworking guy—on my way home from making the money that feeds my daughter and keeps a roof over our heads. Despite all that effort, I am not a full citizen. I'm just a suspect. I'm someone who is not trusted to move about freely. This is the silent reality most black men have to live with. They won't say anything to you at work, it's not a part of their everyday conversation, but this is the reality.

A couple of years later, I started working for marketing companies that were based in the Los Angeles area, but I had to travel back to the Washington, D.C., area frequently. I had officially moved to Los Angeles, so when I traveled to D.C. for any extended period of time, I would rent a room in the house of a family friend for a few weeks. My daughter would stay with me and often played with my friend's three daughters, who lived in the house.

One day, I took all four of the girls out to a park so they could expend some of their energy before the evening. On this particular day, I took them to a park in Adams Morgan, an area that is a fairly upper-middle-class part of northwest D.C. When I go to this park, generally I am the only black male around. Whenever I take the girls to the park, I stand where they are playing and take a book along so that I can read but also look up every so often to check on the children and make sure everything is all right. On this day, I looked up and saw several police cars pulling up to the entrance of the playground. I thought that there must have been a problem down at the other end of the playground where adults and teenagers play basketball. But the police were not interested in that area, they were walking toward me. As the police started to approach, one officer took out his billy club and motioned for me to sit down. I had no clue what could have been the problem. After all, I was just standing with a book in my hand. As the officers stood over me they began to ask me what I was doing. They told me that someone called them and told them that "a black man was in the park watching kids." I told them that I *was* watching kids—my own and my friends'. Just as I said this, the kids ran over to me saying, "Uncle Nii-Odoi/Daddy, what's wrong?" The police then saw that it was a big mistake and started to apologize.

Despite their apology, they seemed unsympathetic to how I felt. They said they were just doing their job. I understood that somebody called them. But in the end it was just another indication that, even when I am watching over children in my care, I am still a suspected miscreant. My freedom is illusory. It is interesting that black men are so highly regulated while corporations steal billions from citizens and usurp resources from poor countries and the planet. I guess black men are the diversions.

One spring, I went to visit my father in New York City. Visiting him is something I do frequently, but I especially love New York in the spring. Since my father had to work during the day, I decided to spend the day walking around and shopping on 42nd Street. As I headed out to chill and enjoy the day, I heard a disturbance behind me. I turned around to see what was happening, and I saw several men running toward me, just like I've seen "jump out squads" do.* They were headed right toward me, and I braced myself for the takedown. I immediately assumed the "regular position" that so many black men are conditioned to know for their survival: I put my hands up and became as quiet and docile as possible. Even though I didn't know for sure if they were cops, I couldn't take the chance, so I was keenly aware of not doing anything that would make me another Amadou Diallo on the eleven o'clock news.

They slammed me up against the wall and then threw me down on the ground. Then they began asking questions. As I was lying on the ground, they asked me for my identification, but would not answer my simple question: "What is this all about?" What this group of men did do is finally identify themselves

---

*"Jump out squads" are a group of undercover detectives in an unmarked car who drive near an area where drug dealers are operating and then quickly jump out of the car to arrest or detain as many suspects as possible.

as police officers. It's thought provoking, to say the least, that civil servants who are charged to serve and protect me end up being the ones I need protection from. In situations like these, I have learned to make my abuser as comfortable as possible. Finally, the cops started telling me that someone was robbed and that I "fit the description." Reading my Washington, D.C., identification, they started questioning me about why I was New York City. Even though this experience is all too common, I wondered whether it was real. Was I in New York or in Israel/Palestine? Do I need papers to move? Was I told that I couldn't move without my papers? Did I miss the roadblocks and checkpoints? I thought this was the United States and that I could move from state to state as I pleased.

I was reminded of the reality that this is the role that so many black men have to play. I'm guilty until proven innocent. My innocence is not presumed, I have to explain it. So I started calmly telling the officers that I was visiting my father; I told them where I was from, and where he worked. I felt that I had to run down my whole life up to this point. To add insult to injury, I was doing this in front of what was now a packed crowd in downtown New York.

As I was finally let go, I tried to shrug off what had happened and continue my day. I tried to dismember that this was yet another strike against my humanity, another assault on my confidence, another chip away from my citizenship. It hit me that I was not to be a protected citizen, but rather that citizens were to be protected from me.

When I arrived back at my father's workplace, I told him what had happened. He reprimanded me for walking around. He told me, "You know you just can't walk around like that." I shrugged off what he said as if he was some guy that wasn't hip to the fact that black people have been "free" for 150 years. But I didn't really believe my own words. Black men are always shrugging off these incidents. It's psychological torment.

Despite all these experiences that had the possibility of ending up in jail, or worse, there was one incident in which I thought I truly might die. It was a nice summer day in D.C., and I, my brother, and a friend were returning from a visit with my father in New York. We were driving my brother's car and had just exited the highway. As we entered downtown D.C., I noticed the police in the rearview mirror. I was braced to get stopped, as I had been countless times before. I knew all my paperwork was in the car and that it was in an accessible place where they wouldn't think I was reaching for a gun. That's something I don't think a lot of other folks have to worry about when they get into a car, but for me, when I get behind the wheel, I don't immediately think about a seat belt or if I have enough gas. Rather, I think, "Do I have all my papers and identification in an open place so that I can give them to a cop without making him think I am reaching for a gun?"

As I expected, the cop turned on his lights and siren and signaled for me to pull over, and I did. The police waited in the car for several minutes. Then, I noticed several other cars pull up. At that moment, the officer in the first car got out and approached our car. Since I already knew the routine, I had my license ready to hand him. He took it, looked at it, and asked why I was driving a car with New York State plates. I said that it was my brother's car, that we were just getting back from New York, and that it was my turn to drive for the last leg of the journey. The officer gave me a suspicious look and returned to his car with my license. In the meantime, even more cars were pulling up—about five now—while pedestrians began to stop and gawk at the scene. After a few more minutes, the officer walked back up to my window and said, "Get out of the car." I asked the officer what was wrong, but he stood there and repeated his command, "Get out of the car." While this was happening, other officers were surrounding my brother's car and looking through the windows as if they had lost something. Then the cop orders all of us out of the car. As we got out, we were all told to put our hands on the car. I was shocked. I could not believe this was happening. Without our permission they began to search the car and told us to stand still with our hands remaining on the hood of the car.

I was getting very upset now. I had to be still, but I did not have to be quiet. I admonished the police about how they were treating us like criminals and how they did not even ask us to search the car or tell us why they stopped us. Just then, out of the corner of my eye, I noticed my friend and brother trying to get my attention. When I looked at them, they gave me this look that said "Shut up!" But I could only think, "No. You both might be timid, but I will not shut up."

One of the officers closed in on me and began yelling for me to "shut my mouth." The other officers also began to move closer and were yelling at me. At that moment, my friend motioned for me to look behind me. When I glanced back, I realized that the source of their fear was a cop pointing his gun at my head. I couldn't believe it. I was so angry. What could we have done to warrant this? I just don't get it. Maybe it is a fear of our potential. After they finished illegally searching the car, they said we could go. When asked why they stopped and searched us, they replied that the windows of the car were too darkly tinted and that they had probable cause.

That brings me to another story. Once again, I was stopped by the police in D.C. The officer told me that my license was suspended and he would have to impound the car. He told me that the rule was that if your license is suspended, then you should be arrested. He said he would give me a break, and I should go get the situation fixed.

I didn't understand. I thought my license was in working order. I went down to the DMV to see about the problem. I was told that there was a prior ticket which did not get processed as paid in full. They fixed the error and gave me a copy of the statement saying that my license was in fact not suspended and that my license was valid. Although I was disappointed that my car had been wrongfully taken, I was happy that this stage of the event was over. Now my challenge was to figure out how I was going to get to the far end of D.C. to pick up my car from the impound lot. The area where my car was kept was in the poorest section of D.C., and the city did not provide a metro rail to get there. So I took the bus to the area, found the impound lot, and retrieved my car.

As I drove down South Capitol Street to get on the parkway, I heard a siren and saw flashing lights in my mirror. I pulled over. The procedure began as it always has: "Here is my license and registration." But I also gave the officer my documentation that my ticket was paid and that my license was not suspended. I sat in the car for what seemed to be an eternity, wondering what the holdup was. The officer finally came back and asked me to step out of my car. What?! I know how this goes. I asked the officer if he had read the DMV document stating that my license was valid. He replied that it didn't matter. His computer in his squad car told him that the license was suspended. End of story.

I got out of the car, and the officer told me to turn around. I pleaded for him to read the document and to let me go. He just became more aggressive in his tone and slapped the cold handcuffs on my wrists. At that point, they might as well have been slave shackles. I sat on the curb as inner-city black families walked by and shook their heads. It wasn't shame that made them shake their heads so much as it seemed to be their realization that this happens all too often.

I was taken to the station and fingerprinted, and I watched as my prints were run through a nationwide fingerprint database. They were checking to see if there was a warrant out for me in another state. I was finally released with no shoestrings in my shoes—police often take shoestrings from those put in jail so you can't harm yourself or others with them. As I walked to the subway train, I ran into an older black gentleman with no shoestrings either. We looked at one another with a painful recognition. Profiling is generation to generation. We were trapped.

In tolerating these transgressions day in and day out, I sometimes feel like my humanity is being chipped away. I feel like that essential quality—the thing that makes me a social creature—is eroding. I wonder if I will ever heal from these events. I wonder if one day they will manifest in a supreme lack of confidence or perhaps a violent reaction. Who knows how these experiences will tally up in my psyche? I'm reminded of what the philosopher Hegel said: "Each of us can know that we are free and independent persons only if we see that others recognize us as free." I wonder when I will really be free.

7

NOTES OF A NATURALIZED SON

Devon W. Carbado

Devon W. Carbado is a vice dean and law professor at UCLA School of Law, where he has twice been elected Professor of the Year and has received both the Rutter Award for Excellence in Teaching and the university-wide Distinguished Teaching Award. A Fletcher Fellow, he, along with Rachel Moran, is editor of Race Law Stories. *His book* Acting Black, Acting White: Working Identity *with Mitu Gulati is forthcoming from Oxford University Press.*

The incidents in the story that follows speak to the inescapable nature of racial profiling in the United States. As a black man from another country, Carbado recounts two baseless police searches that revealed to him a naturalization process outside the official government procedures familiar to many U.S. immigrants. After only a few sobering

lessons in the black-and-white dynamics of police encoun-
ters, he quickly became "one step closer to becoming [a] black
American."

After I had been living in America for about a
year, I purchased my first car: a $1,500 used yel-
low convertible Triumph Spitfire. Two weeks later, my
brother, who had been in the States for under a month,
and I were on our way to a friend's house. It was about
nine P.M. We were in Inglewood, a predominantly
black neighborhood south of Los Angeles, when we
heard a siren and a police car signaled for us to pull
over. One officer approached my window; the other
stationed himself beside the passenger door. He directed his flashlight inside the car, alternating its beam
on our two faces.

"Anything wrong, officers?" I asked, trying to
discern the face behind the flashlight. Neither officer
responded. I inquired again as to whether we had done
anything wrong. Again, no response. Instead, one of
the officers instructed, "Step outside the car with your
hands on your heads." We did as he asked. He then

told us to sit on the side of the curb. Grudgingly, we complied.

As we sat on the pavement, "racially exposed," our backs to the officers, our feet in the road, I asked a third time whether we had done anything wrong. One officer responded, rather curtly, that I should "shut up and not make any trouble." Perhaps foolishly, I insisted on knowing why we were being stopped: "We have a right to know, don't we? We're not criminals, after all."

Today, I might act differently, less defiantly. But, at the time of this incident, my strange career with race, at least in America, had only just begun. In other words, I had not yet lived in America long enough to learn the ways of the police, the racial conventions of black and white police encounters, and the so-called rules of the game: don't do anything. Nothing. Don't talk. Don't move. Nothing—except what the officer explicitly authorizes you to do. Just say yes to whatever the officer tells you to do.

No one had explained these things to me, and they were not intuitive—not to me, anyway. It had not occurred to me that my encounter with these officers was potentially life threatening. This was one of my many racial blind spots. Eventually, I would develop my second sight.

The officer discerned that I was not American. Presumably, my accent provided the clue, although my lack of racial etiquette—mouthing off to white police officers in a "high-crime" area in the middle of the night—might have suggested that I was an outsider to the racial dynamics of police encounters. My assertion of my rights, my attempts to maintain my dignity, and my confronting authority might have signaled that I was not from here and, more importantly, that I had not been racially socialized into, or internalized the racial survival strategy of, performing obedience to the police.

The officer looked at my brother and me, seemingly puzzled. He needed more information to process us racially, to make sense of what he might have experienced as a moment of racial incongruity. While our phenotypical blackness may have been apparent, our performance of blackness could have created a racial indeterminacy problem. That is, to the extent that the officers held the view that our blackness meant we were criminals or thugs, our English accents might have challenged it. However, at best, this challenge was partial. The officer could see—with his "inner eyes"— that we had the souls of black folk. He simply needed to confirm our racial stock.

"Where are you guys from?"

"The U.K.," my brother responded.

"The *what*?"

"England."

"England?"

"Yes, England."

"You were born in England?"

"Yes."

"What part?"

"Birmingham."

"Uhmm . . ." We were strange fruit. Our racial identity had to be grounded.

"Where are your parents from?"

"The West Indies."

At last, we made racial sense. The officers had located our racial roots.

"How long has he been in America?" The officer wanted to know, pointing at me.

"About a year," my brother responded.

"Well, tell him that if he doesn't want to find himself in jail, he should shut the fuck up."

The history of racial violence contained in his words existentially moved us. We were now squarely within a subregion of the borders of American blackness. Our rite of passage was almost complete.

My brother nudged me several times with his elbows. "Cool it," he muttered under his breath. The intense look in his eyes inflected his words. "Don't provoke them."

By this time, my brother needn't have said anything. I was beginning to see the black and white racial picture. We had the right to do whatever they wanted us to do, a reasonable expectation of uncertainty. With that awareness, I simply sat there—quietly. My brother did the same. We were in a state of rightlessness.

Although I didn't know it at the time, we were one step closer to becoming black Americans. Unwillingly, we were participating in a naturalization ceremony within which our submission to authority reflected and reproduced a quintessential black racial experience. We were being "pushed" through the racial body of America to be born again; a new motherland awaited us. Eventually we would become naturalized sons—black American males.

Without our consent, one of the officers rummaged through the entire car—no doubt in search of ex post probable cause; the other watched over us. The search yielded nothing. No drugs. No stolen property. No weapons. Ostensibly, we were free to leave.

One of the officers asked for my driver's license, which I provided. My brother was then asked for his. He explained that he didn't have one because he had been in the country only a few weeks.

"Do you have any identification?"

"No. My passport is at home." We both knew that this was the wrong response.

The officers requested that we stand up, which we did. Pursuant to black letter law, or the law on the street for black people, they forced us against the side of the patrol car. We were spread-eagled, and they frisked and searched us. Still no guns. Still no drugs. Still no stolen property.

The entire incident lasted approximately twenty minutes. Neither officer provided us with an explanation as to why we were stopped. Nor did either officer apologize. By this time, I understood that we were not in a position to demand the latter. The encounter ended when one of the officers muttered through the back of his head, "You're free to go."

"Pardon?"

"I said you can go now."

And that was that. The racial bonding was over (for now). I wanted to say something like, "Are you absolutely certain, Officer? We really don't mind the intrusion, Officer. Do carry on with the search. Honest." But the burden of blackness in that moment rendered those thoughts unspeakable. Thus, I simply watched in silence as they left.

The encounter left us more racially aware and less racially intact. In other words, we were growing into our American profile. Still, the officers did not physically abuse us, we did not "kiss concrete," and we managed to escape jail. Relative to some black-and-blue encounters, and considering my initial racial faux pas—questioning authority and asserting rights—we got off easy.

Subsequent to that experience, I have had several other incidents with the police. I shall recount only one more here.

Two of my brothers and my brother-in-law had just arrived from England. On our way from the airport, we stopped at my sister's apartment, which was in a predominantly white neighborhood. After letting us in, my sister left to run some errands. It was about two o'clock in the afternoon, and my brothers wanted some tea. I showed one of them to the kitchen. After about five minutes, we heard the kettle whistling. "Get the kettle, will you?" There was no answer. My other brother went to see what was going on. Finally the kettle stopped whistling, but he never returned.

My brother-in-law and I were convinced that my brothers were engaged in some sort of prank. "What are they doing in there?" Together, we went into the kitchen. At the door were two police officers. Guns drawn, they instructed us to exit the apartment. With our hands in the air, we did so.

Outside, both of my brothers were pinned against the wall at gunpoint. There were eight officers. Each was visibly nervous and apprehensive. Passersby comfortably engaged in conspicuous racial consumption. Their eyes were all over our bodies. The racial product was a familiar public spectacle: white law enforcement officers disciplining black men. The currency of their stares purchased for them precisely what it took away from us: a sense of racial comfort and safety. No doubt, our policed presence confirmed what the on-lookers already "knew": we were criminals. Why else would the police treat us this way?

The officers wanted to know whether there was anyone else inside. We answered in the negative. "What's going on?" my brother-in-law inquired. The officer responded that they had received a call from a neighbor reporting that several black men had entered an apartment with guns. "Rubbish, we're just coming in from the airport."

"Do you have any drugs?"

"Of course not. Look, this is a mistake."

The officers did not believe us. We were trapped inside their racial imagination. The body of evidence—that is to say, our race—was uncontestable. Our only escape, then, was to prove that, in a social meaning sense, we were not what, phenotypically, we quite obviously were: black.

"May we look inside the apartment?"

"Sure," my brother in-law consented. "Whatever it takes to get this over."

Two officers entered the apartment. After about

two minutes, they came out shaking their heads, presumably signaling that they were not at a crime scene. In fact, we were not criminals. Based on "bad" information—but information that was presumed to be good—they had made an "error." "Sometimes these things happen." At least they were willing to apologize.

"Look, we're really sorry about this, but when we get a call that there are men with guns, we take it quite seriously." (The officer did not say "black men with guns," though likely that is how the neighbor described us.) "Again, we really are sorry for the inconvenience," the officer continued. With that apology, the officers departed. Our privacy had been invaded, we experienced a loss of dignity, and our blackness had been established—once more—as a criminal identity.

But that was our law enforcement cross to bear. The police were simply doing their job: acting on racial intelligence. And we were simply shouldering our racial burden: disconfirming the assumption that we were criminals. No one was really injured. Presumably, the neighbors felt a little safer.

My eyes followed each officer into his car. As they drove off, one of them turned his head to witness the after-spectacle: the four of us racially traumatized in the gunned-down position they had left us. Our eyes met for a couple of seconds, and then he looked away. It was over. Another day in the life, for the police and for us. Simple injustice.

We went inside, drank our tea, and didn't much talk about what had transpired. Perhaps we didn't know how to talk about it. Perhaps we were too shocked. Perhaps we wanted to put the incident behind us— to move on, to start forgetting. Perhaps we needed time to recover our dignity, to repossess our bodies. Perhaps we knew that we were in America with such a welcome. Perhaps we sensed that the encounter portended a racial taste of things to come, and that this experience of everyday social reality for black Americans would become part of our visible lives. Perhaps we understood that we were already black Americans, that our race had naturalized us.

We relayed the incident to my sister. She was furious. "Bloody bastards!" She lodged a complaint with the Beverly Hills Police Department. She called the local paper. She contacted the NAACP. "No, nobody was shot." "No, they were not physically abused." "Yes, I suppose everyone is all right."

Of course, nothing came of her complaints. After all, the police were "protecting and serving." We, like other blacks in America, were the unfortunate but necessary casualties of the war against crime.

8

SEVERED TIES

KENT H.

Kent H. is thirty-five years old and was born and raised in the Bronx, New York. He has worked for several years as a job developer in the nonprofit world and focuses much of his energy on being a good father to his seven-year-old daughter.

The constant harassment by the police Kent experiences, whether he is sitting on a park bench talking on his cell phone, visiting his mother's apartment in a public housing project, or having a conversation with a friend in the lobby of his own building, makes him feel as if he lives in a police state.

One day, I was coming home from where I used to work. I wore a suit and tie to work every day, so that's how I was dressed. There were police in my lobby, and as I was walking through the lobby to get in the elevator, they saw me. They said, "How are you doing?" I replied, "How y'all doing?" Then I headed upstairs. I changed my clothes, threw on some jeans, a T-shirt, boots, and a hat, and I came back downstairs. They had the nerve to ask me if I lived in the building. I told them that I had just come into the building twenty minutes ago wearing a suit and tie. One of them said, "Oh, no, you didn't."

My thought was, *Wow, I put on some different clothes, and now you don't know a brother. Okay.* "Yes, I do live in the building," I said. All I could think was, *I just came in the fucking building like twenty minutes ago, and you saw me!* I repeated, "Yes, I do live in the building." So now he asks me for ID. I showed them my ID. One of the officers tried to take it from me. You see with your eyes and not with your hands. So I said, "No, you asked to see my ID, not take my ID." They called me a smartass, but I was just basing it on what the guy said. They looked at each other and decided to let me go, so I left. I don't know if they were housing police or regular cops. They're all together, to me.

I even have a hard time going to visit my mother. Officially, I live downtown, so my ID has my downtown address. My mother lives in the projects uptown, and I'm not on the lease for my mom's apartment. The police told me that if I was to go there and my mother isn't home, they would arrest me for trespassing—even if I have keys to her apartment, which I do. They said that if I use my key to go into her apartment, they are going to arrest me because my ID says that I don't live there. So I can't visit my mother? Because if I do, and she is not home to verify that I'm her son, they're going to mess with me and probably arrest me for trespassing—with a key.

Just the other week, I went to visit a friend of mine in his building. As I was leaving I was stopped, questioned, and arrested for trespassing because I didn't live in the building. I told the police what apartment I had been in, and they supposedly went to verify it with the tenant. But they knocked on the wrong apartment door, so they decided I was lying and took me in. I had just gotten paid, and I even had the paystub on me. I had $300 cash in my pocket. In the precinct they took $200 and never gave me a voucher, which is what they are supposed to do for any amount above $100. Once I finished going through the whole central booking process, I asked for my money back and they wouldn't give it to me. So I said, "Yo, come on, I know what I had on me." They said they didn't know what I was talking about. And of course I got upset. Then they told me, "Shut the fuck up before we beat your ass." Shut the fuck up? "I want my money! You took my money!" Once you get into the precinct they talk reckless. They say whatever they want, however they want to, and if they want to throw the billy club in your gut, they can do that, too. I've had that happen to me before.

It gets to a point where you can't walk anywhere without these dudes harassing you. You could be sitting in the park by yourself, talking on your cellphone, minding your business. These dudes run up on you and surround you like you're an actual criminal. Last summer, I was in the park doing just that. Some cops walked up to me and asked me, "What are you doing in the park?" I answered, "I'm on the phone."

Now, this is public property. They told me I couldn't be in the park because there's a curfew. Where does it say so? I was sitting behind *my* building in the projects. I wasn't even in a regular New York park. I was in the projects. I was home. There's no sign anywhere around that says there's a curfew in that damn park. I can't sit in there?

Then they asked me, "Do you have anything on you?" Do I have anything on me? Oh, come on, now y'all want to be assholes.

"I don't have anything on me."

"Can I search you?"

"No, you cannot search me."

"Why are you being so resistant?"

"Because, like I told you, I don't have anything on me."

One cop started to grab me, and I started trying to snatch myself away from him. Now they wanna get rough. They flipped me over and threw me on the bench. They were holding me down and searching through my pockets. Then they called for backup. Now there were four more dudes coming down, just for one guy. There were about eight officers in total by the time all the backup arrived. All because I told them I would not let them search me.

I was by myself, on my cellphone, in the park. I wasn't bothering anybody, but they just wanna fuck with me! They don't have anything better to do. So they searched my pockets to make sure I didn't have anything on me, and they were contemplating whether or not they should arrest me. And sure enough, I wound up going to central booking because of that incident. They charged me with resisting arrest and disorderly conduct, which is bullshit. But now I have to deal with the bullshit of going through central booking. You can sit in there for two or three days before seeing the judge. They don't understand how much one little arrest can fuck up a person's life. And not just that person, but the whole family. This is just one time, but I've been in a similar situation about four times. Going through central booking for no good reason becomes routine.

Another time I was in the lobby of my building in the Bronx, talking with a friend, just having a regular conversation. I don't know what went down to cause this, but four DTs [detectives] rushed the building. They screamed, "Get your hands on the fucking wall! Get your hands up; hands on the wall!" From the lobby, they took us into the stairwell and stripped us. Four big white guys pulled down our pants—the whole nine yards. Supposedly because they felt we had drugs on us. They were saying, "We know you got drugs on you. We're going to find 'em."

It was the most embarrassing experience. People were coming in the lobby and they saw this happen.

It was crazy, really crazy. When they realized that we didn't have anything, they just left. No apologies, no "I'm sorry"—nothing, nothing, nothing! They just left us standing there. They walked away, and we put our clothes back on.

I know every month they have a quota to meet: a certain amount of arrests they need to make every month. Some of them haven't met their quotas, so then they arrest dudes just for trespassing or for having a nickel bag of smoke on them.

My general feeling when it comes to police? I hate 'em. They walk around like they rule the whole fucking world, especially the DTs. They act like they are untouchable. There's also a whole level of physical intimidation. Their presence, without even saying anything, says, I'm God—I'm the law. And it doesn't matter whether you've committed a crime or not, everyone is getting messed with by the cops.

I'd be lying if I said that all cops are bad. I've come across some alright cops who understand—those who have either been through it themselves or know someone who's been through it. So they tell you straight up: "Listen, I got a job to do. Do me a favor: when I come back, don't be here. You know they don't want you here." Gotcha. In that case, I give them the respect due. But most of them want to prove that they're a bigger dude. You have a uniform. You have a badge. Come on, that tells it all right there.

At the end of the day, all cops are not bad. But the majority are. Most do their job badly. They go overboard with their job. I liked it better about fifteen or twenty years ago. Back then you had some cops who knew the community, the community knew them, and both sides gave respect. If something went down, knowing that a certain cop is cool, they would let him know—especially if it was affecting the community somehow. But now they are really just dickheads. They abuse their power to the fullest extent. I even feel that they take advantage of all the 9/11 laws to justify messing with us now. They talk about how they don't need probable cause to search you, even though they were doing that before those laws were in effect. That doesn't have anything to do with us; that's terrorist shit, but it gives them free rein. I just try to stay out of their view as much as possible. If I see them walking my way, I walk the other way.

It's crazy. They need another way of policing.

They really do. But truthfully I don't know that they can even do it. The relationship between people and the cops right now is so fucked up. Nobody trusts them. And when you see for yourself how grimy they are, you don't want to deal with them. Truthfully, that's where all the gangs came into play, because they feel like, "Fuck the police." The police aren't really anything more than just another gang. There could be one or two dudes hanging out and then there's a whole fucking precinct on them, just for one or two dudes. Come on. What did he do? He ain't killed no president or nothing like that.

A year or two ago, we had something in our projects where somebody from an organization came and talked to the community or whatever. I went to listen to what they were saying. All these same issues were put on the floor, but then nothing happened. Ain't nothin' changed. Everything is still the same. They [the cops] are still acting up, and niggas are still getting harassed. To be honest, I don't know what they can do. Or what we can do as far as trying to reconnect with them, because that line has been severed so badly. I don't think it can be repaired now. They're just all fucked up.

The situation feels hopeless. I just try to keep my distance from them and just stay away from them. This state is like a police state, truthfully. I'm just waiting for them to say martial law. Once that happens all hell is going to break loose. The bottom line is, if you give us respect, we give you respect. That's all. It's a respect factor. They don't have any, man. They have no respect whatsoever.

9

"DO YOU LIVE IN THIS NEIGHBORHOOD?"

PAUL BUTLER

Paul Butler is a law professor at George Washington University in Washington, D.C. He has clerked for the U.S. District Court in New York and has worked in private practice, specializing in white-collar criminal defense and civil litigation. Butler also served as a federal prosecutor with the U.S. Department of Justice and as a special assistant U.S. attorney, prosecuting drug and gun cases. He is now a leading expert on criminal justice and provides legal commentary for CNN, NPR, and the Fox News Network. He has written for the Washington Post, *the* Boston Globe, *and the* Los Angeles Times, *as well as the* Yale Law Journal, Harvard Law Review, *and* Stanford Law Review, *among other journals. Butler is also the award-winning author of* Let's Get Free: A Hip-Hop Theory of Justice.

In this piece, Butler writes eloquently about his own "Skip Gates moment"—an occasion on which he was made by police to prove his identity on the porch of his own house.

Sometimes, being a scholar of criminal procedure and a black man seems redundant.

I am walking in the most beautiful neighborhood in the District of Columbia. Though I'm coming home from work, I feel as if I'm on a nature walk: I spy deer and raccoons and hear ridiculously noisy birds. And—even more unusual in Washington, D.C.—black *and* white people. Living next door to each other. It's more like Disney World than the stereotypical image of Washington, D.C.

It is the neighborhood where I am fortunate enough to reside, and I am ashamed that the walk is unfamiliar, having been occasioned by my broken car. The time is about nine P.M., and the streets are mostly deserted. When I'm about three blocks from home, a Metropolitan Police car passes by and slows down. I keep walking, and the car makes a right turn, circles the block, and meets me. There are three officers inside. Their greeting is, "Do you live around here?"

I have been in this place before. I know that answering the question will be the beginning, not the end, of an unpleasant conversation—"Where do you live?" "It's kind of cold to be walking, isn't it?" "Can I see some ID?"—that I don't feel like having.

So I ask a question instead: "Why do you want to know?" The three officers exchange a glance—the "we've got a smartass on our hands" glance. I get it a lot.

"Is it against the law to walk on the sidewalk if I don't live around here?" I ask. When no response is immediately forthcoming, I say, "Have a nice evening, officers," and head toward home.

The police now use an investigative technique that probably has a name other than "cat-and-mouse," but that is the most accurate description. They park their car on the side of the road, turn off their lights, and watch me walk. When I pass out of their range of vision, they zip the car up to where they can see me.

In this fashion we arrive on the block where I live. I have a question, and so I stop and wait. For once, I have the power to summon the police immediately, quicker even than the president, who lives about seven miles away. Sure enough, as soon as I pause, the car does too. The police and I have a conversation consisting mostly of questions.

"Why are you following me?"

"Why won't you tell us where you live?"

"What made you stop me?"

"We don't see a lot of people walking in this neighborhood."

"Are you following me because I'm black?"

"No, we're black, too."

The answer is true, but it is not responsive. I ask the officers if they have ever been followed around a store by a security guard. They all say yes. The senior officer—a sergeant—says that it doesn't bother her because she knows she's not a thief.

I ask if that's how the kid in the Eddie Bauer case should have felt. A Prince George County police officer, moonlighting as a security guard, made an African American teenager take off the shirt he was wearing and go home to get a receipt in order to prove that he had not stolen the shirt from the store. Testifying about how that made him feel, the black man-child cried.

The case had been in the news the previous week because a jury awarded the boy $850,000. Nonetheless, the sergeant says she isn't aware of it.

The officers tell me that they're suspicious because this is not a neighborhood where they usually see people walking. Furthermore, they know everybody who lives in the neighborhood, and they don't know me. I ask if they know who lives there, pointing down the road to the house where I have lived for fourteen months. Yes, they answer; yes, they do.

And so I walk. I walk up my stairs. I sit on my porch. I wait. I wait because I am a professor of criminal procedure. I wait because I remember the last time, with different officers, in a different place, when I "cooperated." Which meant that I let them search my car. Or rather, I let one search while the other watched me. With his hands resting near his gun. On 16th Street. Cars whizzed by. I pretended that I was invisible.

Now the officers park their car and position its spotlight on my face. All three of them join me on my porch.

"Do you live here?"

"Yes, I do."

"Can we see some identification?"

"No, you may not."

During the antebellum period of our nation's history, blacks were required to carry proof of their status, slave or free, at all times. Any black unsupervised by a white was suspect. In North Carolina, to make it easier for law enforcement, non-slave blacks had to wear shoulder patches with the word "free."

The District of Columbia, through its three agents standing on my porch, tells me: "If you live here, go inside. It's too cold to be out."

I am content where I am. So, the police announce, are they. They will not leave me until I produce some ID or enter the house.

I have arrived home late because I worked late, writing about a book for the *Harvard Law Review*. The book, which I'm carrying in my knapsack, is *Race, Crime, and the Law*, by Randall Kennedy. Since apparently none of us has anything better to do, I take the book out of my sack and show the officers Chapter 4, "Race, Law and Suspicion: Using Color as a Proxy for Dangerousness." The chapter contains several stories just like this one. It quotes Harvard Professor Henry Louis Gates Jr.:

Blacks—in particular, black men—swap their experiences of police encounters like war stories, and there are few who don't have more than one story to tell. Erroll McDonald, one of the few prominent blacks in publishing, tells of renting a Jaguar in New Orleans and being stopped by the police—simply "to show cause why I shouldn't be deemed a problematic Negro in a possibly stolen car." The crime novelist Walter Mosley recalls, "When I was a kid in Los Angeles, they used to spot me all the time, beat on me, follow me around, tell me that I was stealing things." Nor does William Julius Wilson wonder why he was stopped near a small New England town by a policeman who wanted to know what he was doing in those parts. There's a moving violation that many African-Americans know as D.W.B.: Driving While Black.

But this, I announce, is the first time I've ever heard of "walking while black." I point to the big window of my beautiful house. I tell the police that I have seen people, mostly white, walking down the street at all times of the day and night, and I have never heard them questioned about their right to be there. That is why I will not show them my identification. This is not apartheid South Africa, and I don't need a pass card.

The officers are not interested. In fact, they announce, they're getting angry. There have been burglaries in this neighborhood and car vandalism. The police are just doing their job, and I, *I*, am wasting the taxpayers' money. One officer theorizes that I'm homeless. Another believes that I am on drugs. The one thing of which they are certain is that I don't live in the house attached to the porch on which I am sitting. And when they find out who I "really" am, I will be guilty of unlawful entry, a misdemeanor. "Another night of overtime," they note with satisfaction.

The sergeant tells me that, since I'm being "evasive," she will interview my neighbors. The two remaining officers radio for backup. They give the dispatcher the wrong address, and I correct them. Soon, a second patrol car, with two more officers, arrives. I am cold but stubborn.

Finally, my neighbor comes outside and identifies me. I'm free now—free to be left alone. Free to walk on a public street. Free to sit on my porch, even if it is cold.

But first, we—the five law enforcement officers and I—look to my neighbor for vindication, a moral to justify the last hour of our lives. My neighbor is black like us. He says that he is always happy to see police patrolling the neighborhood. But, he adds, many white people walk here late at night, and they are not questioned about their right to be there. My neighbor tells the officers that they are always welcome to stop by his house for coffee, and he goes home. The sergeant invites me to a crime prevention meeting at the police station in a few weeks. Then, the five officers get into their two cars and drive away.

As for me, I'm still searching for a moral. My neighborhood does not seem so beautiful anymore. I get my car repaired right away; I enjoyed the walk, but I dread the next set of officers. Sometimes, I prefer to leave criminal procedure at the office. Sometimes I like a walk to be simply a walk.

But sometimes I am willing for my walk to serve as a reminder, for the police and for you, reader, about the Fourth Amendment and its protection against unreasonable government intrusion. If I had a television show, I would say, "Kids, don't try this at home." It is unfortunate, but other uppity Negroes have gotten themselves shot for less than what I did. The officers I encountered were professionals, even if the male officers were not especially polite. They never led me to believe that they would physically harm me or even falsely arrest me. It is sad that I should feel grateful for that, but I do.

One reason that I felt safer with the officers was because they were African American. They might stop me because I'm black, but I didn't think they would be as quick on the draw as nonblack officers, who are more susceptible to prejudice. The black officers' construct of me—a black man walking in a neighborhood where people don't often walk at night—was a *burglary suspect*, a *homeless person*, or a *drug addict*. The white officers' construct—even during a traffic stop— would have been a *violent black man*. At least that is what is communicated by the standard procedure: the approach with the hand on the gun, the order to exit the car, and the pat-down search. This doesn't occur every time, but often enough.

Because the officers were black, I was especially angry. They should've known better.

What is reasonable law enforcement? Like my neighbor, I had been pleased to see police patrols—at least until the police patrolled me. Still, I could excuse the intrusion as the price of life in the big city if everybody had to pay the price. But everybody does not. Ultimately, my protest is less about privacy and more about discrimination.

Most courts say that police may consider race in assessing suspicion. It is probably true that there are more black than white burglars and car thieves in D.C. In *United States v. Weaver*, 966 F.2d 391 (1992), the U.S. Court of Appeals for the 8th Circuit said of racial profiles:

> [F]acts are not to be ignored simply because they may be unpleasant. . . . [R]ace, when coupled with other factors [is a lawful] factor in the decision to approach and ultimately detain [a suspect]. We wish it were otherwise, but we take the facts as they are presented to us, not as we would like them to be.

But the fact is that most of the black people who walk in my neighborhood are, like me, law-abiding. And the fact is that some white people are not law-abiding. Race is so imprecise a proxy for criminality that it is, in the end, useless.

The police officers made me an offer before they left. If I wanted to know when they stopped white people who walked in my neighborhood, they would tell me. They would ring my doorbell any time, day or night, to let me know.

Ironically, considering the officers' lack of interest in Professor Kennedy's book, their offer is also his suggestion. Kennedy believes in colorblindness, including in assessments of suspicion. He writes:

> [I]nstead of placing a racial tax on [minorities], government should, if necessary, increase taxes across the board. . . . [It] should be forced to inconvenience everyone . . . by subjecting all . . . to questioning. The reform I support, in other words, does not entail lessened policing. It only insists that the costs of policing be allocated on a nonracial basis.

I turned down the offer, thinking that the police might begin to question every walker in my neighborhood just to make a point. That would not make me feel any safer, and it would inconvenience the neighbors.

In retrospect, I made the wrong decision. I hadn't wanted to draw the enmity of my neighbors by causing them to be treated like criminal suspects—or like black men. Sometimes the law gets me confused about the difference. Kennedy is correct: It is a confusion everyone should share.

10

LOOK HOMEWARD, ANGEL

JOSHUA T. WILEY

Joshua T. Wiley holds a GED and is currently studying to become a teacher. He is a burgeoning hip-hop artist by the name of "RAW," and he is affiliated with the group Top Souljas. He has worked an array of jobs and is father to a son named Caleb and a daughter named Ariel. He splits his time between Clarksville, Tennessee, and Asheville, North Carolina.

Here Wiley recounts a particularly egregious example of blatantly prejudiced and violent behavior on the part of the Asheville, North Carolina, police that constitutes but one episode in what Wiley calls "my profiled life."

I am a black man who grew up in Asheville, North Carolina. For many people today, Asheville is known for its "progressive" and "liberal" spirit. People who have this narrow and romanticized vision of a white, hippie, 1960s place flock to this town. These days, it's not uncommon to walk on a downtown street in Asheville and catch a whiff of patchouli mixed with marijuana or to see signs advertising a yoga studio that specializes in healing crystals. This Asheville is not the Asheville I grew up in. I grew up in the neighborhood of Montford in the 1980s and 1990s. Then, before it was declared a "historic district"—which consequently drove up property taxes and resulted in an overnight influx of middle-class and rich white folks to the neighborhood—it was a majority black and lower-class area. I grew up just a few blocks from a house where squatters lived. Nowadays, it's a bed-and-breakfast. A former crack house is now a European bistro.

Montford is wedged among the predominantly black housing projects of Klondike and Hillcrest, Interstate 240, and UNC–Asheville. Of note, Montford also contains Riverside Cemetery, the resting place of Asheville native and author Thomas Wolfe. Wolfe lived in Asheville at the dawn of the twentieth century, and many agree that his writings were autobiographical reflections of his own experiences in Asheville.

I bring up Wolfe for two reasons. First, whenever I leave Asheville, I feel as though I am drawn back toward it. It's like I must "look homeward," as the title of Wolfe's most famous book goes. Second, when I return to Asheville, I am reminded, like another Wolfe title, that I "can't go home again." I feel drawn toward Asheville in order to recover my childhood; Asheville, no matter how rough it was, was still the place of my beginnings and my childhood. It was my home. And yet, I can never seem to reclaim it. The home I look for is no longer there. What I find instead is a harsh reality: Asheville, despite its supposed progress and growth, can be an unforgiving and hostile place for her black native sons like me.

Since attending high school in the nineties, I went on to get my GED. I have lived in a few other places, most notably in Clarksville, Tennessee. I've held several jobs. Most recently, I was a factory worker in Clarksville and, after being laid off, I returned to Asheville in November of 2009 to search for work. I got a job working as a cook in a small restaurant on Merrimon Avenue. But the boss refused to give me more than a few hours per week, so I quit that job and began to look elsewhere. Finding a job is never an easy task for a black man. Combine that with my level of education and the "Great Recession," and it's even worse.

I do find success with my music. I belong to a hip-hop group named Top Souljas. I perform several times a week, sell my CDs, and work on albums and music videos. Despite the bad economic situation, I'm anything but complacent. I support myself through hard work and my music.

That said, in October 2009, I met up with my friend whom I'll call "John," also a young black man, and another whom I will call "Chris," who is a white guy. I knew both John and Chris from other jobs, and we did our best to get together every few weeks to hang out, catch up, and enjoy the parts of life that we could. On this one night, we decided to go to a club in downtown Asheville because John had received a promotional flyer for that evening. The flyer allowed us access to the club without a cover charge and gave each person—up to four people—one free beer.

From the get-go, I wasn't too excited about this club. It was known for being a fairly white club. Now, don't get me wrong, there's nothing wrong with folks enjoying their time with whomever they want to, but many folks of color know that when a place is marked explicitly as "white," they are not just talking about the numbers, but rather about how much people accept folks with my complexion and hair texture. Given my hesitation, I was happy that Chris, as the white guy, was going with us.

We waited until about nine o'clock in the evening and headed downtown. The walk was a quick one, as the club is only about a mile from my grandmother's house. We walked up to the door and showed the bouncer our promotional flyer. He looked us up and down suspiciously. He kept glancing back and forth from the flyer to me, John, and Chris. Finally, he gave us back the flyer and told us to go inside and enjoy our night. We walked in and I was ready to have some fun—feeling as though dealing with the jerk of a bouncer/doorman would be the only hurdle of the evening. In just a few minutes, I found out I could not have been more wrong.

Upon adjusting my eyes to the relative darkness of the club, I quickly scanned the room. "Nope, just me and John," I thought. We were the only two black people in the club whom I could readily identify. "Well, that's what I expected," I thought to myself. We all remarked that we were thirsty and walked over to the bar. Chris, who was now holding the promotional flyer for the free beer, gave the flyer over to the barkeeper and put up three fingers to denote that we each wanted a beer. "You boys got ID?" the barkeeper asked. Now, I'm a thirty-two-year-old man, I have short dreadlocks, and my features hardly qualify as a "babyface." And, both John and Chris are older than I and look it. I rarely get carded, and I rarely get called "boy" unless someone is trying to make some point about my status. Still, I brushed it off and reached into my front pants pocket, where I keep my wallet. (I never keep my wallet in my back pocket—a habit conditioned from years of being around folks who need to take advantage of wallets peeking out of the back pockets of unsuspecting people.) "Just give me my drink," I thought.

I handed the barkeeper my driver's license, and so did John and Chris. The barkeeper gave us the same look as the bouncer outside: his eyes danced back and forth between us, our IDs, and the flyer. He studied these documents for what seemed like a minute until finally Chris asked, "Is there a problem?" The barkeeper looked up at him and said, "Yeah, there's a problem; we don't take coupons." "Whoa. It's not a 'coupon,'" said

John. He continued, "A girl gave me the flyer earlier today—she was doing promotions for you guys. That's why we're here." The barkeeper just stared at John for a few seconds and then repeated as if John were slow. "Like. I. Said. We. Don't. Take. Coupons." "It's not a damn coupon!" Chris yelled at the bartender. "It's your own damn flyer. You gonna honor it or not?"

At this point, I was pissed off with the bartender *and* with Chris. The bartender was obviously a jerk and didn't want to serve us. But Chris—he knew better. Here we are in this club, around all these white folks, with a bouncer and a bartender who apparently have a problem with us, and you—the white guy—are going to start getting loud?

The bartender looked to the back of the room and motioned for someone to come over. "Good," I thought. "Bring the manager over and let's get this handled." I waited for some white guy in a tie to walk over and ask "What seems to be the problem?" and imagined him leading us to a table before he all gave us our drinks and an apology. I was awakened from this fantasy when a large bouncer came over and grabbed John by the arm. "Okay boys, time to leave." he grunted at John. John's eyes became wide. "What?

We're not even doing anything," John replied. "We just want a beer."

The bouncer remained calm as he gripped John's arm just beneath his armpit, forcing him to the door. "Come on, you guys are out of here," he said. Chris and I both protested as we followed John and the bouncer to the door. At one point John said, "Okay, Okay. We're leaving, just take your hands off me." But the bouncer just moved more quickly with John to the door. Another bouncer came up behind Chris and me and motioned us out the door as well.

We rushed out into the cold night air. Even though it's North Carolina, Asheville is in the mountains, and nighttime Asheville air in January is frigid. I remember looking though the fog of my breath as it blew through the night air. The bouncer pushed John away from the door just as we came out. John yelled at the bouncer not to push him and that it was unnecessary since we were already outside and were not resisting getting kicked out from the club.

As luck would have it, a uniformed cop standing by the sidewalk of the club walked over to John, and with his hand on his holstered gun, yelled at John to "calm down." John yelled something, I couldn't tell whether it was at the cop or the bouncer, but the cop grabbed John, forced him to the ground, and told him to put his hands behind his back. I remember yelling, "You don't need to be rough with him. We're already leaving."

The next thing I know I'm waking up in the middle of the parking lot. The cold January Asheville air on my exposed genitals brought me back to consciousness. I tried to get up, but my hands were cuffed behind my back. My head was aching, and I felt a burning sensation on my face, chest, and legs—evidently scrapes from hitting the pavement and being dragged along, unconscious, on the asphalt of the club's parking lot. My shirt was torn, and my pants and underwear were pulled down to my knees. I could see a crowd of white people encircling me, watching the situation unfold. In that moment, my mind raced to images of lynchings that were used as postcards for most of the early 1900s. The white crowd was calm and serene, just like in those photos. It had always perplexed me how a white crowd could stand there emotionless around the body of a lynched, disfigured, burned, and brutalized black man. It hit me that the faces in those photographs were the same faces staring at me now. Jim Crow has a timeless and frozen expression.

I was brought back to the present by the embarrassment that my pants were down. I was literally exposed to the world. As the cop brought me to my feet, I am sure I gave that white crowd quite a show, even as the cop tried to pull up my pants and provide me some measure of respect. Ironic that now he seemed to care about my dignity as a man. The cobwebs from my head were clearing, and I began to try to reason through what just happened. The last thing I remembered was telling the cop to leave John alone, I told him that we were leaving, and I told him that we didn't want trouble.

It was only later that I found out what happened from John and Chris. Evidently, I was struck on the back of my head by the cop's partner and was tackled to the ground immediately following the blow. I don't remember falling or even being hit. I don't know if it was his fist, a billy club, or something else—I still don't know to this day. I do know that I had a massive knot on my head and, days later, I had to go to urgent care because of severe pain in my neck and back. The doctors told me I had a broken bone in my neck and severely pulled ligaments in my neck and upper back. They told me that, fortunately, such a break was minor and that my injuries would probably heal, although I might continue to experience bad headaches and even spasms in my neck and back. I would be fine, they told me.

As I think about that night, I recall being lifted up by the cop and noticing that John was in the back of another car. He stared at me through the glass. I didn't see Chris anywhere, although he told me he was there watching and yelling my name. I don't doubt it, but I guess I just was a bit out of it. I was searched again on the hood of a police car by another cop and eventually placed in the backseat. After a few minutes of sitting there, another cop got in the car and drove me less than a mile or so to the police station.

The police station in downtown Asheville is right next to city hall, the county courthouse, and the jail. Just behind the police station is a historically black area of town. As I was being driven though that area—an area where I had walked many times, an area where I attended parties at the YMI Cultural Center, an area where I used to get my hair cut at the barber shop on Eagle Street—I thought of Wolfe's racist description of that same area in *Look Homeward, Angel*. It was an area he described as "Niggertown":

It was as dark as night, as evil as Niggertown, as vast as the elemental winds that howled down across the hills: he chanted it in the black hours of his labor, into the dark and the wind. He understood; he exulted in its evil—which was the evil of earth, of illicit nature. It was a call to the unclassed; it was a cry for those beyond the fence, for rebel angels, and for all of the men who are too tall. (p. 252)

It was at that moment that I understood how those cops and bouncers really saw John and me. I have been profiled many times in the past. I've applied for jobs in writing or over the phone, having been told that the position was open, yet when I showed up for the interview, the position was suddenly filled. I've been pulled over numerous times by cops and asked if I have any "guns" or "drugs" in my possession. I've been followed through stores even when I have cash in my pocket. I live a profiled life. I know how it feels to be a "problem." But on that night, my skull throbbing from the cop's blow to my head, as I looked out through the glass of the police cruiser to gaze upon Wolfe's "Niggertown," I realized something. Even though

Asheville has changed so much that I can hardly recognize it anymore, one thing remains the same—it is still racially segregated, and it probably will remain that way for some time. The color line will endure as long as black men are understood as "evil," "unclassed," of an "illicit nature," and belonging to the area "beyond the fence" still known as "Niggertown."

But I am no rebel angel. I just wanted a drink with my friends. My only crime was being black in a white club. My offense was asking for the same opportunities as the club's white patrons.

I was taken into the station, processed, and put in a cell. I asked all the officers—the one who drove the car, the one who booked me, and the one who placed me in the cell—what I was doing there, and I received no answer. I remember pleading with the cop who placed me in the cell, "Just tell me what I am being arrested for. What are the charges?" He replied, "You'll figure all that out tomorrow. Maybe someone will come and bail you out." I told him in return, "Do I get to call anyone to tell them that I am here?" I heard no response except the clank of the door. I sat there, replaying what happened, over and over again. I wondered if John or Chris were also there with me, in another room somewhere. I wondered if they might have gotten word out to my sister, to my cousins, to a friend, or to anyone who could come and get me out. I wanted to sleep—just go to sleep to get through the night. I wanted to sleep and wake up to see a friend standing there. But I was too uneasy to sleep, especially since I was not the only one in the cell—folks were brought in and out all night. Most were drunks and would fall asleep, pass out, or yammer on to me about how they were arrested unfairly. "Unfairly?" I thought. They had no idea.

The next day a cop came and told me I was free to go. I asked for my belt, shoes, and wallet, which were all taken from me the previous night. They gave me my shoes and belt and told me I didn't have a wallet when I was brought in. I protested, but to no avail. I remember putting my ID in my wallet after I got it back from the bartender and placing my wallet back in my front pants pocket. They told me to leave or that I would be arrested again. I asked them what I was "arrested" for in the first place, and they said I was held "for my own safety."

I've since made a formal complaint to the Asheville Police Department about the "alleged" incident. I have been told that the officer who allegedly "tackled" me was reprimanded, but I was not told who he was or what punishment, if any, he received. I asked for an official apology, but was told there was no alleged wrongdoing. They repeated the answer even after I asked why an officer was "reprimanded" if there was no wrongdoing. I was informed that there was no official record of either my "arrest" or the "incident." I went back to the club and talked to the bouncers from that night. They told me that they had no idea why the cops jumped on John and me, or why Chris was so mysteriously overlooked.

Most recently, I left Asheville and returned to Clarksville, Tennessee. I still look homeward, but then I remember that I can't go home again.

11

NOT GIVIN' IN

M.K. ASANTE

M.K. Asante is an award-winning author, filmmaker, and professor. He is the author of the books It's Bigger Than Hip-Hop; Beautiful. And Ugly Too; *and* Like Water Running Off My Back, *as well as the feature documentaries* The Black Candle, 500 Years Later, *and* Motherland. *He is an associate professor in the Department of English and Language Arts at Morgan State University.*

Asante's piece offers a chilling picture of the kind of disaffection that can be engendered by racially biased police practices.

"If you try to tell the people in most Negro communities that the police are their friends, they just laugh at you."

> —Dr. Martin Luther King Jr.

"Fuck the police."

> —Traditional Saying

The scene: a calm, star-spangled sky suspended above Philadelphia like the snatch of silence before a great storm. This moment of clarity was fitting because, just hours earlier, on Flatbush Avenue in Brooklyn, I interviewed the rappers of Dead Prez about their altercation with, and subsequent civil suit against, the notorious NYPD. Even amid a hip-hop landscape overrun with toxic waste, Dead Prez has been an unflinching beacon of light, critically exposing, among myriad other contributions, the police brutality that occurs routinely in black and Latino communities. In their song "Police State," they rap:

> The average black male
> Lives a third of his life in a jail cell.

Instead of *protecting and serving* the community, these cops *served* Dead Prez with nightsticks and handcuffs. Dead Prez responded, in part, by retaining the legal services of Brooklyn-based activist and attorney Karl Kamau Franklin in hopes of using the System against itself. One wonders, though, as I did driving though "the city of brotherly love" on my way home, if this could really be done. Wasn't this a case of running to the wolf to tell on the fox? Wasn't it Audre Lorde who proclaimed, "The master's tools will never dismantle the master's house"? That while "they may allow us temporarily to beat him at his own game, they will never enable us to bring about genuine change"? Or, perhaps as in the work of all great artists, there was something else—something greater, something deeper, something more knotty—at work here. And I began to see, as I drove up the battered blocks of North Philadelphia, the black face of Caliban, the slave from Shakespeare's *The Tempest* who was taught, by brute force, the bloody language of Prospero, his oppressor. Caliban, in turn, used Prospero's language to curse him, just as Dead Prez sought to do now.

I was almost home when I, too, was blinded by Prospero's blood red and cold blue flashing lights and deafened by his high-pitched gulp of a cry—*Woop-woop! Woop-woop!* I pulled my car over and came to a full stop in front of a check-cashing spot and a thin storefront with a handwritten sign that read OFF THE CHAIN BAIL BONDS.

Possible (not probable) causes cascaded through my mind—*Maybe my brake lights are out. . . . Maybe my tag's expired. . . . Damn, maybe I didn't pay those parking tickets. . . . Nah, I paid them*—as a cop approached my car, crushing gravel beneath his bulky boots.

"Problem?" I asked, as a pale, paunchy man whose eyes were veiled with tinted shades arrived at my door.

"Where you coming from?" the officer questioned.

"Brooklyn," I told him as I scanned his tag—L. CLARK—into my memory.

"Brooklyn?" he said, surprised. "What's in Brooklyn?" I knew that, because of the Fifth and Sixth Amendments, I wasn't obliged to answer his questions, but because I wanted to get home as soon as possible, I did.

"I was conducting an interview," I said plainly.

"License and registration," he requested as

his eyes, chasing the orb of his flashlight, searched through my car.

"It's in the glove compartment," I stated.

"Slowly," he warned.

My hands, moving in calculated slow motion, floated toward the glove compartment when—"I said slow!" the cop screeched, as he grabbed the handle of his Glock. "Unless you want to get shot!" His voice harshened.

At that moment, I came to the pungent realization—just as so many, too many, before me have—that this already tragic encounter could very easily conclude with that gun, which his pink hand was now molesting, being tugged out of its dark nest, aimed at me, and fired multiple times into my black body. What's worse is that this outcome, which was not at all uncommon, was beyond my control. If I followed his instructions, he might, overwhelmed by an unwarranted but very real fear, imagine my wallet or cellphone to be a gun and shoot me. If I didn't follow his instructions, then he would certainly send shots my way. Either way, because of my hue and, indeed, his, he had carte blanche. With my back against the wall, I knew, as James Baldwin did when he inked *A*

Dialogue, that "he's got a uniform and a gun and I have to relate to him that way. That's the only way to relate to him because one of us may have to die."

My fingertips and palms, moist with the anxiety of sudden death, handed him my license and registration.

"Why was I stopped?" I asked.

"Hold tight," he said, as he took my papers and turned around.

"Why was I stopped?" I repeated as he wobbled back to his squad car.

I watched him, through the sharp panorama of my mirror, as he ran my papers. I was reminded of the armed white men, dubbed "pattie rollers" by African Americans, who were deployed throughout the South to patrol and prevent slave rebellions. These patrols, which white men in the South were required to serve in, operated exclusively at night, traveling on horseback from plantation to plantation, harassing black people, looking for contraband (weapons, liquor, books, etc.) that might indicate a plan to flee. Pattie rollers were instructed to lash viciously any enslaved African without a written pass. In North Carolina, a law ordered pattie rollers to whip on the spot any "loose, disorderly, or suspected person" found among enslaved Africans. It was from these pattie rollers, funded by local taxes, that many modern policing concepts were derived. For example, pattie rollers, like modern police, referred to patrollers' designated areas of operation as "beats."

Everything came back clean. No tickets. No warrants. No nothing.

"Do you have any drugs or weapons in the car?" the officer asked.

"You still haven't told me why I was stopped," I stressed.

"One more time. Do you have any drugs or weapons?" he repeated, resting his hand on his gun (again).

"I've got a registered handgun and a permit to carry it," I stated.

I felt his demeanor morph, and I could see from the involuntary breach between his cold lips that he wanted to say something. I anticipated him asking me, "Why are you brandishing a firearm?" And I anticipated telling him that although I hate guns—and never have liked them, not even as toys—I was overcome just a few weeks prior with the awful feeling of not being able to save my own life. The trigger for me was when Sean Bell, twenty-three, an unarmed black man and father of three children, was shot in a vicious hail of fifty bullets on the night before his wedding.

I'd made up my mind that I was not going out like Patrick Bailey, the twenty-two-year-old unarmed black man shot and killed by twenty-seven NYPD bullets. Or Amadou Diallo, the twenty-three-year-old unarmed black man who was shot forty-one times and killed by four plain-clothed NYPD officers. Or Abner Louima, another unarmed black man who was beaten by the NYPD and then sodomized by Officer Justin Volpe with the filthy handle of a toilet plunger, severely rupturing his colon and bladder, before Volpe jammed the excrement-soiled stick down Louima's throat, damaging his teeth, gums, and mouth. Mos Def, during the Diallo trial, asked, "At this rate, can we expect the hail of fifty-five bullets to be unloaded on another New Yorker by next fall?" He reminded folks that "this is not a black issue; it's a human issue."

I thought about the family of Artrell Dickerson, the eighteen-year-old boy who was gunned down by Detroit police during a funeral, just a few weeks after

Bell's murder. Dickerson's family, in a passionate statement that is a challenge to all of us, wrote:

I charge you to prove that the actions of this officer (who still remains anonymous) were justified. I charge you to prove that Artrell's death was not over-kill, that he did not die face down on the ground with as many as six bullets in him on a cold Monday afternoon, in broad daylight, with up to a hundred men, women, and children as witnesses to murder. I charge you to prove to this community that black men are not being killed indiscriminately in the city of Detroit at the hands of police officers whose crimes are being covered. Until then we will not be silenced because we are empowered in our belief that Artrell's death is characteristic of many other killings of African American men in inner cities across the United States at the hands of police officers. And we wish to inform and empower the public to demand the respect and protection of the lives of our brothers, cousins, fathers, uncles, and friends. Artrell Dickerson will not have died in vain.

I decided that, unlike Bailey, Diallo, Louima, Bell, Dickerson, and countless others, I would not be unarmed, and that if they shot at me, I would shoot back with everything I had. The logic: if white police officers love their families as much as we love ours, then knowing we are armed as well, perhaps they will think twice before they shoot us. "As the racist police escalate the war in our communities against black people, we reserve the right to self-defense and maximum retaliation," former Black Panther leader Huey Newton said while incarcerated on bogus charges. And this wasn't just rhetoric; Newton saved his own life by firing back at Oakland police officers when they attempted to assassinate him in 1967. Similarly, Tupac Shakur, in 1993, shot two off-duty police officers who were harassing him and a black motorist. When it was discovered that the cops were drunk and in possession of stolen weapons, all charges against Tupac were dismissed.

We must never mistake the self-defense of the victim for the violence of the attacker. Self-defense is not an act of violence, but rather an act of self-love and self-preservation. In 1919, when a thick brush of race riots swept across the country like wildfire, Harlem

Renaissance poet Claude McKay responded with "If We Must Die," a poem urging blacks to fight back. McKay's poem, written nearly a century ago, spoke to me now:

> If we must die, let it not be like hogs
> Hunted and penned in an inglorious spot,
> While round us bark the mad and hungry dogs,
> Making their mock at our accursed lot.
> If we must die, O let us nobly die,
> So that our precious blood may not be shed
> In vain; then even the monsters we defy
> Shall be constrained to honor us though dead!
> O kinsmen we must meet the common foe!
> Though far outnumbered let us show us brave,
> And for their thousand blows deal one
>   deathblow!
> What though before us lies the open grave?
> Like men we'll face the murderous, cowardly
>   pack,
> Pressed to the wall, dying, but fighting back!

The officer didn't ask me why I had a gun; he had something else in mind.

"You don't mind if I take a look around, *do ya?*" The officer slurred as he opened the door.

"Actually, officer, I don't consent to a search of my private property," I informed him, myself informed by a fairly good understanding of my Fourth Amendment rights, which state:

> *The right of the people to be secure in their persons, houses, papers, and effects against unreasonable searches and seizures shall not be violated, and no warrants shall issue, but upon probable cause, supported by Oath or affirmation and particularly describing the place to be searched and the persons or things to be seized.*

"You hiding something?" the officer pried.

"No," I said flatly, "I'm exercising my Fourth Amendment right against unreasonable searches and seizures." I knew that according to the Plain View Doctrine, he could only initiate a search if an illegal item was in plain view and that the only reason he was asking me to consent to a warrantless search was because he didn't have enough evidence to search without my consent. I also knew that, from both common sense and previous experiences, just because a law is on the books, its application is much less clear, especially where race is concerned. After all, in 1857, the U.S. Supreme Court ruled in *Dred Scott vs. Sandford* that blacks "had no rights that white man was bound to respect." But this didn't deter me from asserting my rights because, in that same year, Frederick Douglass warned:

> *Find out just what the people will submit to and you have found out the exact amount of injustice and wrong, which will be imposed upon them; and these will continue until they are resisted with either words or blows, or with both. The limits of tyrants are prescribed by the endurance of those whom they oppress.*

So, in an attempt to limit his tyrannical oppression, I refused to submit. As Ras Baraka explained on The Fugees' sophomore album *The Score*, "Cuz if you let a mothafucka kick you five times, they gonna kick you five times. But if you break off da mothafucka's foot, won't be no more kickin'."

"Step out of the car," the officer ordered as he opened my door.

"You still haven't told me what I was pulled over for. What was I pulled over for?" I insisted.

Completely ignoring my question, he says, "What are you hiding, boy?"

"Boy?"

"Fuckin' nigger," he vomited.

At that moment, I was faced with two distinct choices: life or death.

This is exactly his plan, I chuckled to myself as I chose life. *He wants me to flip. He wants me to flip. Nope I'm not givin' in. Not givin' in*, I told myself, attempting to prevent my blood from bubbling, desperately trying to prevent the death, which was waiting above the scene like a vulture, from occurring.

"I know my rights," I insisted, to which he threw my license and registration into my car and stalked off, frustrated at his impotence.

In France, the black and Arab youth scream, *"Police partout, justice nulle part!"* meaning "Police everywhere, justice nowhere." So long as officers like L. Clark patrol neighborhoods in a predatory manner, there will be no justice—can be no justice.

Although the racist, hostile, and violent attitudes police officers display in cities across America present a real problem, the new generation mustn't be short-sighted in analyzing and solving this age-old conflict. Just as we cannot blame the teachers who are put in crumbling, overcrowded schools for the education problem or the soldiers on the ground in Iraq for the war, we must be committed to working our way up the ladder of power. It is there—among the decision makers—that the problems that plague all of us are preserved and maintained. Despite the anger that we may feel toward police, it is not guns that will save our collective lives, for they never have and never will. Instead, it is organizing in such a way as to attack the injustice at its roots and save the lives of our unborn children and grandchildren. Most important, it is up to us to imagine a new system—a system not rooted in the past of America's slavery days, but in the freedom of tomorrow.

12

STAND!

KING DOWNING

King Downing is an attorney and director of the Human Rights–Racial Justice Center. Formerly the national coordinator of the ACLU's Campaign Against Racial Profiling, Downing worked with the organization's affiliates and partners to identify and end racial disparities in policing on the federal and local levels. He has led "Know Your Rights" workshops and has spoken on criminal justice in many settings across the country.

Downing's piece demonstrates that not even experts on the topic of racial profiling are exempt from being profiled. It also documents an exemplary response and advocates powerfully for taking a public stand against this insidious practice.

*   *   *

For the moment the pressure was off. I stepped into the fresh air. The automatic door slid shut behind me. Now I had some space between myself and the state trooper who just had ordered me out of the airport.

That I was a tall black man was obvious to the trooper. What was not obvious was that I was a Harvard-educated lawyer and the national coordinator of the American Civil Liberties Union (ACLU) Campaign Against Racial Profiling and that what he was doing to me seemed to come right out of the police practices playbook that we were advocating against.

The ACLU, an organization with hundreds of thousands of card-carrying members, had worked, for almost a century, to protect people and organizations from government violations of the Constitution's Bill of Rights: freedom of speech and religion; due process of law; equal protection regardless of gender, race, ethnicity, nationality or sexual orientation; reproductive freedom; legal representation; and protection against cruel and unusual punishment.

The organization was wrongly painted as a bastion of liberalism, as if constitutional rights were not the birthright of people across the political spectrum. Many times, the ACLU had represented people and organizations from the Right who felt that the government had violated their rights. Ask conservative radio host Rush Limbaugh. After years of attacking the ACLU from behind his media ramparts, he embraced the organization to represent him when his drug abuse medical records were wrongfully made public.

The goal of my project was to focus on the police, due process, and equal protection. The shorthand word was "racial profiling," where police take action based not on individual suspicion but on race, ethnicity, or, especially after 9/11, religion or country of origin. My project also focused on situations where the police did have individual suspicion but decided whether or not to investigate or enforce the law based on the same criteria. The campaign's work involved public education, legislation, litigation support, outreach, and media awareness.

I stepped away from the terminal with strong, careful strides. As I reached the curb I looked out for a taxi, hoping one would pull right up and get me away from there.

One day earlier, I had flown from Seattle to Boston on a "red-eye" flight from the West Coast. I just had left a convention of representatives from over forty nations of indigenous people (who call themselves "Indians"). I was there to make a presentation on racial profiling as a national problem and an Indian problem, and to help create awareness and solutions. My investigation had found that racial profiling in Indian country was serious. Among the Lakota and Dakota nations in South Dakota, we documented problems in three tribal areas.

For example, in the town of Martin, near the reservation, the Lakota told me that sheriffs targeted Indians and ignored whites in traffic stops, searches, and DWI (driving while intoxicated) arrests. Indians were given Breathalyzer tests even while walking. They also charged that sheriffs waited outside Indian bars at closing time to catch DWIs, but never waited outside white bars. Some sheriffs, too impatient to wait until closing time, went into bars and demanded IDs on the spot, checking for traffic warrants and setting a new low for unconstitutional efficiency. The Lakota charged that the sheriffs stepped up these practices each month right after the Lakota had received their Bureau of Indian Affairs checks. These were monthly payments to individual tribal members as compensation for the government's historic taking of their lands.

We had organized a community meeting which the U.S. Department of Justice attended. What was the Lakota solution? They held a voter registration drive, turned out to the polls in force, and voted in an Indian sheriff. Soon after, the two worst deputies quit.

My relief didn't last long. The terminal door slid back open. I heard the heavy footsteps of authority closing in fast behind me.

I had left the Indian meeting in Seattle that night right after the event because I had a racial profiling meeting with community and advocacy groups at ten o'clock the next morning in Boston, Massachusetts. Then, I was scheduled to leave at six o'clock that night to return to Seattle to do workshops and take tribal complaints all day, because the larger part of the Indian attendees were scheduled to arrive for the weekend after driving from all over the country. Very few outsiders come to them, they said. They needed me to come back. Jet-lagged or not, I couldn't say no.

In Boston, I was a participant in the racial profiling working group of the Executive Office of Public Safety (EOPS). In the wake of years of complaints of widespread racial profiling, Massachusetts had passed a law banning the practice and requiring the reporting of traffic citation and search statistics. All departments with significant racial disparities would have to collect an additional year of stop-and-search data.

The working group, put together by Northeastern University for EOPS and made up of community members, advocates, and police, met monthly to review the data and recommend the findings and format for the report. There was a lot of open, honest conversation, but it goes without saying that, at times, the conversation got heated. There was a lot at stake for community and police alike, given that police were aware that the report might cause them to have to collect data for the extra year. In the end, 249 of the state's 366 police departments had to do just that.

But this trip was to meet with community members and advocates to report on the working group, strategize around upcoming meetings, and plan racial profiling solutions. So, as I arrived at around seven o'clock in the morning, I was energized. I had slept on the plane. We had landed on time. Time was tight, but I was on schedule.

With my back to the trooper, as he got closer I wondered: is he in attack mode—ready to grab, tackle me, or worse? And what might happen if I turned around?

You may wonder why I was in a state of concern about racial profiling and police brutality over a simple back-and-forth with an officer over identification. But a Gallup poll reported that an overwhelming majority of blacks (and a smaller majority of whites) believe that racial profiling exists. After reviewing the data from scores of stop-and-search studies covering over half of the 100 largest U.S. cities, I can confirm the existence of racial profiling that people of color have claimed for years.

The U.S. Department of Justice gathered statistics indicating people of color are disproportionately killed or Tasered during encounters with law enforcement. It is not a leap of faith (or lack thereof) that people of color, finding ourselves in similar situations, might also believe that we too were at risk of racial profiling, injury, or death. Consider:

Did Jonny Gammadge, a young black man, have any inkling that he was about to die in Pittsburgh after police stopped him while he was driving a Jaguar that belonged to his uncle, who played for the NFL's Pittsburgh Steelers? Did Sean Bell, Trent Benefield, and Joseph Guzman, on the eve of Sean's wedding night in 2006, have any sense of foreboding as they sat in a van preparing to leave his bachelor party? Undercover New York City police officers, reportedly not showing badges or identifying themselves, and possibly intoxicated, were about to riddle their van with fifty shots, killing Sean and wounding his friends. Les Paultre, father of Sean's fiancée, said, "I went to bed planning a wedding, and woke up to plan a funeral."

If it is acceptable, rational human behavior to play the lottery, hoping to win against great odds, should it be irrational human behavior to anticipate racial profiling or an attack by police, even at great odds? I have called it PTSD—*Pre*-Traumatic Stress Disorder—but there is nothing disorderly about the emotion.

While I could not have put my feelings into so

many words with the trooper bearing down on me, this was my stress level at the time.

"I told you I want to see some ID," he said as he caught up to me.

"No, you told me that if I didn't show you ID I'd have to leave the airport, so I'm leaving the airport."

"Now I want to see some ID."

Now I was confused. The trooper had told me to show ID or leave, and I had left. Had he really been giving me a choice or was the "choice" a threat to get me to do what he wanted? We had just had this conflict over identification inside the terminal, and I thought it was over.

After arriving in Boston, I had left the plane and walked out of the secure area to a cluster of pay phones by the street-side terminal windows to check my messages. The phones were close to the outer wall of the terminal. My back faced that wall.

A short time after I picked up the phone, I glanced over my shoulder and saw the trooper standing barely an arm's length away to my right, back against the wall, staring straight ahead. "Is there a problem?" he asked. "I'd like to know why you're standing so close to me while I'm on the telephone," I replied. Without losing a beat, he jumped into action. "All right, show me some ID," he demanded in the firm voice police use when showing authority. My mind was jolted. Was this really happening? "I'm not showing you ID. Why do I have to show you ID?" He repeated his order and upped his tone. "I want to see some ID now." "I'm not showing my ID. Why do I have to show you ID? What was I doing?" The back-and-forth continued for several rounds. Each time his command tone got louder and stronger.

Here, I had flown overnight from the West Coast, where I had spent the day hearing emotional stories, and I had gotten off the plane ready to get on with what was going to be a challenging day. My head was spinning. Now I was in the same situation I had talked to tens of thousands of people about on the streets, in classrooms, in workshops, and at town hall meetings across the country. I was in the very situation I had in mind when my project had distributed hundreds of thousands of Racial Profiling Survival Kits in person, by mail, and online. Each envelope contained a know-your-rights "bust card," toll-free hotline sticker, racial profiling fact sheet and comic strip, and Bill of

Rights bookmark. Many of the events have included role-playing to give people a real feel for the situation and to offer them chances to practice their responses to police.

As in the ancient saying, the teacher was now the student.

The trooper kept ordering, and I kept refusing. His command tone rose, but I made sure that mine stayed the same. I had gotten too many complaints by people who had said that the increasing tone of their frustration and even anger at being illegally questioned, stopped, or searched had led to their false arrests. It had become clear that police often "jumped the gun," morphing questions or protests into imagined assaults, leading them to arrest complainers, sometimes beating, Tasing, and even killing them.

I started moving away from him, stepping around the circle of phones. He followed me by going around the other side. As he demanded and I refused, I asked him why I needed to show ID. I never got an answer. I moved into the intersection between the terminal entrance and the parallel walkway, and the trooper followed me. By now, a crowd had started to build. Their faces looked shocked—as if seeing something surreal, as if they couldn't decide between the fascination of real-life drama and the instinct of self-preservation telling them to move on quickly before something serious happened. The trooper changed his approach. "If you don't show me ID, you'll have to leave the airport."

And so, as I said earlier, I left the terminal, and he pursued me out to the sidewalk.

I again refused to show ID. We went back and forth on this a couple more times. At this point I thought it was important to identify the trooper for future reference in case the situation got worse. The problem was that his police ID name tag was turned around. I couldn't read it. Not only was his ID turned around but the clip on which it hung from his clothing was attached backward. Had he purposely reversed his ID? He was either absent-minded or trying to be anonymous. How ironic was it that the trooper, required to display his identification, was demanding mine, which the law did not require showing?

"If you don't show me ID, you're going downtown." I knew what that meant. He wasn't trying to save me cab fare—it was a threat. I took that to mean that I would be arrested and locked up. As I had done in the terminal, I started to walk away from him. He told me to stay where I was. "Am I under arrest?"

"Yes."

Now the situation was way out of control. I had heard these stories so many times, and now I was in the middle of one. "On what charge!!?" "I don't have to tell you that." He stepped back and spoke into the radio microphone hanging on his jacket. I couldn't hear what he said, but a few minutes later three other troopers showed up. They surrounded me. If there had been any doubt, it was clear now—I was *not* free to go.

I passed the time trying to keep alert but cool. I looked at the troopers' faces and name plates (unlike The Trooper, they had small metal name plates correctly pinned to their fronts). I decided to do a little detective work of my own. I told one of the three troopers that The Trooper's name tag was turned around so I couldn't read it. With a straight face he replied that the wind probably had gotten it. In a private thought, I guessed that the wind probably turned the clip around, too.

Sometime later, a trooper, Sergeant Kiley, arrived, surveyed the scene, and stepped off with The Trooper.

The sergeant then came over to me alone. "My officer says you were acting suspicious."

"What did he say I was doing that was suspicious?"

"I didn't ask."

"You're his supervisor, and you didn't ask him what I was doing that was suspicious?"

"He's been with me for years. If he says you're suspicious, you're suspicious." Case closed. How many meetings had I attended where police supervisors assured me that they were "no nonsense" or "zero tolerance" when it came to their officers and rights violations?

Sergeant Kiley told me that if I didn't show ID I'd be placed on a watch or trespass list and would be banned from the airport. Now I was facing a dilemma: continue to refuse and possibly be arrested—"taken downtown"—or put on some list that might keep me from flying back out that night, or who knows what. Either way, I would miss the racial profiling meeting I had crossed the country for, and also miss my return to Seattle, where I had promised the Indian leaders I would return to work with the second wave of people driving to Seattle from all across the country.

I decided to take one for the team. I took out my ID and gave it to Sergeant Kiley. He handed it to The Trooper, who went to a patrol car and appeared to call in my information. He came back to me and handed me my ID. Right at that moment I had the high point of this very low morning—The Trooper's name tag was now properly clipped and facing outward! "Trp. William Thompson" was the mother lode of information I needed to carry out one of the main action items of my workshops:

Complain when your rights are violated.

Thompson gave me back my identification. Just as I thought all this was finally finished and I was ready to move on, they had one more trick up their sleeve. Now they wanted to see my plane ticket, so we went through another round. "I showed you my ID, I'm not going to give you my ticket." They told me again that if I didn't show my ticket they were going to put me on some kind of list that would ban me from the airport.

It was getting late, time was getting short for my meeting, so I decided to take another one for the team—I showed them my ticket. They looked at my

171

ticket and got into a long conversation with each other about whether my ticket, dated the day before, was valid proof that I had legitimate business on October 16th. Finally, they figured out that my ticket was for the day before because I had flown in overnight from Seattle and arrived that morning. If things hadn't been so serious, it would have been a scene from a sitcom.

After a few more unpleasantries, I left Logan Airport, but not before the troopers tossed sarcastic comments my way. But now I had Trooper William Thompson's name. Don't get mad—get even!

At some point before or after the advocates' organizational meeting I told Carol Rose, executive director of the ACLU of Massachusetts, what had happened to me at Logan Airport. Eventually I also met with her and John Reinstein, the organization's legal director. Reinstein wrote a letter to the Massachusetts State Police complaining about Trooper Thompson's behavior toward me and requesting documents. We received a reply from the state police claiming to have no records of any contact with me and refusing to provide any documents, claiming security concerns. We were left with no choice but to take legal action.

Six months after the incident, I filed suit against

the Massachusetts State Police, the individual troopers involved, the trooper who had trained them, and the Massachusetts Port Authority ("Massport"), the agency in charge of the airport. I was represented by the ACLU of Massachusetts and cooperating attorney Peter Krupp. The suit charged that the defendants had violated my rights against unreasonable search and seizures because I was illegally detained by Trooper Thompson and others at Logan Airport and was required, under threat of arrest and prosecution, to show my identification and travel documents. The suit also charged that my unlawful stop, questioning, arrest, and detention were part of a policy that directed police at the airport to question and remove people based on behavior profiles even where there was no reasonable suspicion that the person had done anything wrong.

This charge referred to a passenger screening program, started in 2003 by the airport and the state police, called Behavior Assessment Screening System (BASS) program. This program, which was different from the usual screening all passengers go through at airports, was based on a new concept, "elevated suspicion," which was, according to the state police training materials, "[m]ore than a hunch but less than

[the] reasonable suspicion required to detain a person for criminal investigation."

Under the BASS program "[r]efus[ing] to answer questions or provide identification or travel documents" in response to "voluntary" requests was evidence of "elevated suspicion." And the BASS program said that anyone with "elevated suspicion" should be barred from or escorted away from "critical infrastructure," including the Logan Airport terminal.

From our point of view this new "elevated suspicion" was completely illegal. The U.S. Supreme Court in *Terry v. Ohio* said that a stop based on a guess or a hunch was unconstitutional, and that the requirement to detain a person was at least a "reasonable suspicion." Anything less than reasonable suspicion, including "elevated suspicion," violated the rule in *Terry* and would be a violation of rights.

Finally, the case went to trial. We had settled the claim against Trooper Thompson, but the jury would still have to rule on whether what he had done violated my rights and was required of him under the BASS program. On a cold, wet, miserable evening in December, we waited for the verdict. After what seemed like an eternity the jury came back into the courtroom. Their decision: Trooper Thompson had violated my rights. Victory!

But, not so victoriously, the jury also found that state police training and the BASS program were *not* the cause of Trooper Thompson's actions. The jury might have believed him when he said that he wasn't using the BASS training when he did what he did to me. I didn't.

After the case ended, I felt strong relief and an even stronger sense of justice. I felt relief because it was finally over. This case had been following me wherever I went around the country. Now, a race- and gender-diverse jury of my peers had believed me. I felt justice as I thought about all the people across the country in the same situation who wanted to "just say no" when it came to "voluntary" contacts with the police. I thought of the young men and, increasingly, women of color, some with one or two strikes against them, who were never believed after going through the same thing I went through; not just by police, but by prosecutors, judges, civilian review boards, and even defense lawyers and family—"You must've done *something* wrong."

I don't want to get melodramatic, but I hope that in some small way this might bring relief to all of them. When all this happened, I didn't try to "pull rank" or "get a pass" by announcing that I was a "professional" and a lawyer who was working for a prominent rights organization. I didn't say, "Do you know who I am?" because I wanted to see how Thompson and his associates would treat an everyday person.

Stokely Carmichael was the co-founder of the Student Nonviolent Coordinating Committee (SNCC), the organization of young black men and women whose sit-ins and boycotts broke the back of Southern segregation in the early 1960s. Forty years ago, he said something that is as true today as it was then: *The time is past for description. The time is now for prescription.*

It's not enough to talk about police abuse; we have to "do something" about it. Here is a short list of action items. Do what you can. Adjust the list and your actions based on the conditions where you are:

Know your history and present condition.
Know your rights, teach others, and stand up for
   your rights.

File complaints.

Take legal action, even if you represent yourself.

Join an organization; join and form coalitions.

Reach out to the community.

Survey your community for problems and
solutions.

Hold public events, vigils, and protests; commem-
orate important dates.

Use the media, or make your own, including social
media.

Meet and lobby public officials.

Use open records laws to collect information and
report it.

Observe violations and participate in Copwatch
and Courtwatch.

> Stand! In the end you will be you
> One that's done all the things you've
> set out to do
> Stand! There's a cross for you to bear
> Things to go through if you're going anywhere
> —Sly Stone

ACKNOWLEDGMENTS

We would like to thank Laura Murphy and Janet Peros of Wachtell, Lipton, Rosen & Katz for their expeditious legal assistance, and Tara Grove, Sarah Fan, Reginald Fluellen, Solomon Moore, and Alexander Papachristou for their valuable support in putting this book together. A special thank you goes to Marc Favreau, who came up with the idea for *12 Angry Men*, and to our editor, Diane Wachtell, for making it all happen. Most importantly, we would like to thank all of the contributors for their willingness to share their personal experiences in our effort to expose the dehumanizing reality of racial profiling.